W9-ANU-164

	DATE DUE	

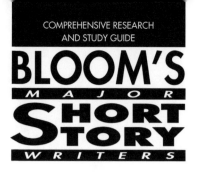

COMPREHENSIVE RESEARCH
AND STUDY GUIDE

BLOOM'S
MAJOR
SHORT
STORY
WRITERS

J.D.

Salinger

EDITED AND WITH AN
INTRODUCTION BY HAROLD BLOOM

CURRENTLY AVAILABLE

BLOOM'S MAJOR DRAMATISTS	BLOOM'S MAJOR NOVELISTS	BLOOM'S MAJOR POETS	BLOOM'S MAJOR SHORT STORY WRITERS
Aeschylus	Jane Austen	Maya Angelou	Jorge Luis Borges
Aristophanes	The Brontës	Elizabeth Bishop	Italo Calvino
Bertolt Brecht	Willa Cather	William Blake	Raymond Carver
Anton Chekhov	Stephen Crane	Gwendolyn Brooks	Anton Chekhov
Henrik Ibsen	Charles Dickens	Robert Browning	Joseph Conrad
Ben Johnson	William Faulkner	Geoffrey Chaucer	Stephen Crane
Christopher Marlowe	F. Scott Fitzgerald	Sameul Taylor Coleridge	William Faulkner
Arthur Miller	Nathaniel Hawthorne	Dante	F. Scott Fitzgerald
Eugene O'Neill	Ernest Hemingway	Emily Dickinson	Nathaniel Hawthorne
Shakespeare's Comedies	Henry James	John Donne	Ernest Hemingway
Shakespeare's Histories	James Joyce	H.D.	O. Henry
Shakespeare's Romances	D. H. Lawrence	T. S. Eliot	Shirley Jackson
Shakespeare's Tragedies	Toni Morrison	Robert Frost	Henry James
George Bernard Shaw	Marcel Proust	Seamus Heaney	James Joyce
Neil Simon	John Steinbeck	Homer	Franz Kafka
Oscar Wilde	Stendhal	Langston Hughes	D.H. Lawrence
Tennessee Williams	Leo Tolstoy	John Keats	Jack London
August Wilson	Mark Twain	John Milton	Thomas Mann
	Alice Walker	Sylvia Plath	Herman Melville
	Edith Wharton	Edgar Allan Poe	Flannery O'Connor
	Virginia Woolf	Poets of World War I	Edgar Allan Poe
		Shakespeare's Poems & Sonnets	Katherine Anne
		Percy Shelley	J. D. Salinger
		Alfred, Lord Tennyson	John Steinbeck
		Walt Whitman	Mark Twain
		William Carlos Williams	John Updike
		William Wordsworth	Eudora Welty
		William Butler Yeats	

COMPREHENSIVE RESEARCH
AND STUDY GUIDE

BLOOM'S
MAJOR
SHORT STORY
WRITERS

J.D.
Salinger

EDITED AND WITH AN INTRODUCTION BY HAROLD BLOOM

© 1999 by Chelsea House Publishers, a subsidiary of
Haights Cross Communications.

Introduction © 1999 by Harold Bloom

Printed and bound in the United States of America.

First Printing
3 5 7 9 8 6 4 2

Library of Congress Cataloging-in-Publication Data

J.D. Salinger / edited with an introduction by Harold Bloom.
p.   cm. — (Bloom's major short story writers)
Includes bibliographical references and index.
ISBN 0-7910-5120-X
1. Salinger, J.D. (Jerome David), 1919-   —Criticism and
interpretation. 2. Short story. I. Bloom, Harold. II. Series.
PS3537.A426Z67 1998
813'.54—dc21
98-41379
CIP

Chelsea House Publishers
1974 Sproul Road, Suite 400
Broomall, PA 19008-0914

CONTRIBUTING EDITOR: Elizabeth Beaudin

Contents

User's Guide

This volume is designed to present biographical, critical, and bibliographical information on the author's best-known or most important short stories. Following Harold Bloom's editor's note and introduction is a detailed biography of the author, discussing major life events and important literary accomplishments. A plot summary of each short story follows, tracing significant themes, patterns, and motifs in the work, and an annotated list of characters supplies brief information on the main characters in each story.

A selection of critical extracts, derived from previously published material from leading critics, analyzes aspects of each short story. The extracts consist of statements from the author, if available, early reviews of the work, and later evaluations up to the present. A bibliography of the author's writings (including a complete list of all books written, cowritten, edited, and translated), a list of additional books and articles on the author and the work, and an index of themes and ideas in the author's writings conclude the volume.

~

Harold Bloom is Sterling Professor of the Humanities at Yale University and Henry W. and Albert A. Berg Professor of English at the New York University Graduate School. He is the author of over 20 books and the editor of more than 30 anthologies of literary criticism.

Professor Bloom's works include *Shelley's Mythmaking* (1959), *The Visionary Company* (1961), *Blake's Apocalypse* (1963), *Yeats* (1970), *A Map of Misreading* (1975), *Kabbalah and Criticism* (1975), and *Agon: Toward a Theory of Revisionism* (1982). *The Anxiety of Influence* (1973) sets forth Professor Bloom's provocative theory of the literary relationships between the great writers and their predecessors. His most recent books include *The American Religion* (1992), *The Western Canon* (1994), *Omens of Millennium: The Gnosis of Angels, Dreams, and Resurrection* (1996), and *Shakespeare: The Invention of the Human* (1998).

Professor Bloom earned his Ph.D. from Yale University in 1955 and has served on the Yale faculty since then. He is a 1985 MacArthur Foundation Award recipient and served as the Charles Eliot Norton Professor of Poetry at Harvard University in 1987–88. He is currently the editor of other Chelsea House series in literary criticism, including BLOOM'S NOTES, BLOOM'S MAJOR POETS, MAJOR LITERARY CHARACTERS, MODERN CRITICAL VIEWS, MODERN CRITICAL INTERPRETATIONS, and WOMEN WRITERS OF ENGLISH AND THEIR WORKS.

Editor's Note

My Introduction raises the question as to whether Salinger's short stories are not period-pieces, even though they continue to attract young readers of what is now a very different era.

The Critical Views excerpted in this volume rarely abound in perceptiveness, but that may reflect the limitations of the stories themselves. Of the general views, the best seems to be that of Peter Buitenhuis, who helps explain why Salinger was not more prolific.

On individual stories, I recommend Ihab Hassan, Warren Erench, David Seed, Alfred Kazin, Joan Didion, and John Updike, all of whom maintain a sensible balance between admiration for Salinger's brilliance of style, and critical misgivings as to the lasting importance of his concerns.

Introduction

HAROLD BLOOM

J. D. Salinger's principal achievement is *The Catcher in the Rye* (1951), a short novel that has attained a kind of mythological status in the nearly half-century since its publication. His short stories, in book form, constitute three equally slender volumes: *Nine Stories* (1953), *Franny and Zooey* (1961), and *Raise High the Roof Beam, Carpenters and Seymour: An Introduction* (1963). Salinger has been silent for the last 35 years, a silence that seems only to have enhanced his popularity. Fresh generations of the young continue to find something of themselves in his work.

Rereading Salinger's 13 principal stories, after a third of a century, is a mixed experience, at least for me. All of them have their period-piece aspect, portraits of a lost New York City, or of New Yorkers elsewhere, in the post-World War II America that vanished forever in the "cultural revolution" (to call it that) of the late 1960s. Holden Caulfield and the Glass siblings charm me now—though sometimes they make me wince—because they are so archaic. Their humane spirituality, free of dogma and of spite, has to be refreshing as we drift toward the millenium.

Of the six stories to which this volume is devoted, "Raise High the Roof Beam, Carpenters" now reads best, not for its "religious pluralism" (as one critic characterized it) but simply for high good humor. Its representation of being stuck in a Manhattan traffic jam has an exuberance that Salinger rarely manifests either in his persons or his plots. Zaniness rather than Zen-Taoist pluralism saves the story from Salinger's inverted sentimentalities and from Glass sibling affections, too frequently emotions in excess of their objects. Salinger's ear for dialogue, inherited from Hemingway and Fitzgerald, is acutely manifested throughout a bizarre narrative in which little happens, which is to be preferred to Seymour's suicide in "A Perfect Day for Bananafish," or Franny's fainting fit in the story that bears her name.

Salinger's stylistic skills are beyond question; his stories perform precisely as he intends. And they hold up as storytelling, even if their social attitudes and spiritual stances frequently now seem archaic or quaint. Their problem is that the Glass siblings are not exactly memorable as individuals. Even poor Seymour is more a type than a vivid consciousness in himself. "Seymour: an Introduction" I find impossible to reread, partly because his brother Buddy, the narrator, never knows when to stop, and again who can tolerate this kind of smug spirituality? Seymour once said that all we do our whole lives is go from one little piece of Holy Ground to the next. Is he *never* wrong?

A reader might well retort: when is Seymour right? The accuracy of Seymour's mystic insight is not the issue. Stories must have narrative values, or they cease to be stories, and "Seymour: an Introduction" fails to be a story. That may be why Salinger's fiction stopped. Contemplation can be a very valuable mode of being and existence, but it has no stories to tell. ❁

Biography of
J. D. Salinger

Jerome David Salinger was born in New York City on January 1, 1919. He lives today in rural New Hampshire, shunning all public attention. Although "Salinger sightings" are reported frequently in magazines and on the Internet, and rumors occasionally circulate that Salinger is about to publish again, seclusion seems to be the milieu this very popular, very private writer prefers.

Little is known about Jerome Salinger's early life. His father, Sol, was Jewish; his mother, born Marie Jillich, of Scots-Irish descent, changed her name to Miriam when she married Sol. His only sibling, a sister, Doris, was born eight years before him. Between 1932 and 1934, he attended the McBurney School, in Manhattan, but did not complete his studies there. In 1936, he was graduated from the Valley Forge Military Academy, in Wayne, Pennsylvania, near Philadelphia. Some critics claim that his years at Valley Forge were the source for some of the material in *The Catcher in the Rye*. Although some similarities exist, the connections between Salinger's novel and his own school days remain at best superficial.

After traveling in Europe in 1938, Salinger attended a course in short-story writing at Columbia University taught by Whit Burnett, then editor of *Story* magazine. Salinger's first published story, "The Young Folks," appeared in 1940, in *Story*. In 1942, at the beginning of the Second World War, he was drafted into the U.S. Army. He attended the Officers, First Sergeants, and Instructors School of the Signal Corps and was later transferred to the Army Counterintelligence Corps. During the Normandy invasion, on June 6, 1944—known as D-Day—he came ashore at Utah Beach with the Fourth Division; later, stationed in Europe, he was security agent for the Twelfth Infantry Regiment. When the war ended, in 1945, Salinger was discharged from the Army. He was married, briefly, to a French doctor named Sylvia; they divorced in 1946.

Salinger wrote much throughout the war years. From 1945 on, Salinger's stories were appearing in print regularly, most often in *The New Yorker*. "A Perfect Day for Bananafish," published during this period, first introduces the character Seymour Glass, who appears later in "Seymour: An Introduction." Darryl F. Zanuck, a producer at 20th Century-Fox, acquired the rights to "Uncle Wiggily in Connecticut," another story that was published in *The New Yorker,* and in 1949 made *My Foolish Heart,* starring Susan Hayward. Hayward was nominated for an Academy Award for her role as Eloise; the film, however, has little to do with Salinger's story.

In 1950, *The New Yorker* published Salinger's "For Esmé—with Love and Squalor," to favorable reviews. By now, Salinger had acquired a reputation as a writer of short fiction. He received an offer from Harcourt Brace, in New York, to publish *The Catcher in the Rye,* but withdrew his manuscript when he encountered problems with the editorial staff; it was published the following year by Little, Brown. The novel won critical and popular acclaim and was on the *New York Times* best-seller list for seven months. Salinger wanted desperately to maintain his privacy, but the success of his book was forcing the creator of Holden Caulfield reluctantly into the limelight.

To escape publicity, in 1953, Salinger moved to New Hampshire. He married Claire Douglas on February 17, 1955. Their daughter, Margaret Ann, was born on December 10, 1955; their son, Matthew, was born on February 13, 1960. In 1967 the Salingers were divorced. Other than an interest in Eastern philosophy, little else is known about Salinger's private life.

Salinger continued to publish fiction from his self-enforced isolation in New Hampshire. When *Franny and Zooey,* which appeared as separate short stories in *The New Yorker,* was published in book form by Little, Brown, in 1961, it was an immediate success. Two other stories, "Raise High the Roof Beam, Carpenters" and "Seymour: An Introduction," also appearing first in *The New Yorker,* were published in book form, in 1963. Salinger's last published short story, "Hapworth 16, 1924," appeared in *The New Yorker* on June 19, 1965; it is scheduled for publication in book form, for the first time, in 1998. Except for denouncing *The Complete Uncollected Stories of J. D. Salinger,* which contains the stories that were published in magazines other than *The New Yorker,* in 1974, and for suing Ian Hamilton and Random House for publishing his unauthorized biography, in 1987, J. D. Salinger remains a virtual recluse. ❀

Plot Summary

"A Perfect Day for Bananafish"

This story was published in *The New Yorker* on January 31, 1948. It became the first story in Salinger's collection of short fiction published under the title *Nine Stories*, in 1953.

Probably the most critically acclaimed of the nine, "A Perfect Day for Bananafish" is in two parts. The first is a telephone conversation between Muriel Glass and her mother; Muriel is speaking to her long-distance from a resort hotel in Florida. Waiting for her telephone call to be put through, Muriel fills her time by reading a magazine article entitled "Sex is Fun—or Hell." "A girl who for a ringing phone dropped exactly nothing . . . she looked as if her phone has been ringing continually ever since she had reached puberty."

Muriel tries to allay her mother's fears about Muriel's husband, Seymour Glass. Her mother is worried because of Seymour's history of mental instability. She carefully explains that Seymour was able to drive them to the resort in Florida without incident, which briefly calms her mother. Her mother then insists on knowing the pet name Seymour is now calling Muriel. Unable to change the subject, Muriel confesses, giggling, that he calls her "Miss Spiritual Tramp of 1948." Muriel is distracted over the book of German poems Seymour gave her, which she has not read ("He said I should've bought a translation or something. Or learned the language, if you please"); she needs to know where the book is in case Seymour asks her.

Describing a consultation between Muriel's father and Dr. Sivetski, a psychiatrist, Muriel's mother provides information on Seymour's past. He was hospitalized while in the Army, released too early according to Sivetski, and now "may completely lose control of himself." Muriel adds that the hotel psychiatrist commented on Seymour as well, which makes Muriel's mother even more worried. A tenuous balance between high anxiety and the commonplace remains throughout this part of the conversation as both women trade remarks on fashion, the hotel room, and the other guests at the hotel. Despite her mother's admonitions that Muriel take the hotel psychiatrist's advice, Muriel continues to maintain that all is well. She seems more troubled by her sunburn than by Seymour's mental condition.

In the second part, Seymour, pale and dressed in a terry bathrobe, is sitting on the beach. Sybil Carpenter, the four-year-old daughter of a hotel guest, has escaped momentarily from her mother's bidding to direct her attention to "See more glass," as she calls Seymour. Seymour's behavior seems normal with the child: He engages her in conversation and participates in her fantasies. They discuss Sybil's dislike of Sharon Lipschutz, another little girl at the hotel. Sybil explains that she likes to chew candles. Seymour helps Sybil to float in the water.

During their conversation, Seymour explains the story of the bananafish to Sybil. According to Seymour, these very ordinary-looking fish swim into a hole filled with bananas. Once inside the hole, the fish go wild. "Why, I've known some bananafish to swim into a banana hole and eat as many as seventy-eight bananas. . . . Naturally, after that they're so fat they can't get out of the hole again. Can't fit through the door." When Sybil asks what happens to the bananafish, Seymour replies, "Well, I hate to tell you, Sybil. They die." Sybil announces an oncoming wave. As they play in it, Sybil shouts that she saw a bananafish with six bananas in its mouth. Seymour picks her out of the water and returns her to the shore. Saying goodbye, Sybil runs back to the hotel.

Returning to his room, Seymour accuses a woman in the elevator of looking at his feet; shocked, she gets off at the next floor. Seymour sees Muriel asleep on one of the beds. Then he takes out the gun from his luggage. "He cocked the piece. Then he went over and sat down on the unoccupied twin bed, looked at the girl, aimed the pistol, and fired a bullet through his right temple."

∾

"Uncle Wiggily in Connecticut"

Originally appearing in *The New Yorker* on March 20, 1948, this story was also included in *Nine Stories*.

The past and the present divide this story, as do the imagined and the real. Mary Jane has arrived for a visit to the Connecticut home of Eloise, an old college friend. In fact, Mary Jane is driving to Connecticut to bring her boss, who is home sick in bed, his correspondence, and decides on the way to drop in on her old friend. Soon the two begin drinking and reminiscing. They both left school before graduation: Eloise was found with a soldier in her dormitory room, Mary Jane married a soldier who was jailed for stabbing an M.P. They drink and gossip about their former classmates.

As Ramona, Eloise's young daughter, enters the room, Mary Jane spills her drink. Her remark that Ramona resembles her mother displeases Eloise, for Ramona wears thick glasses. Eloise insists instead that Ramona looks like her husband, Lew. Mary Jane fusses over the little girl and insists on a kiss. "I don't like to kiss people," Ramona balks. Eloise presses her to tell Mary Jane about Jimmy Jimmereeno. At first, Mary Jane thinks Jimmy is Ramona's boyfriend; she soon realizes, with his green eyes, black hair, no freckles, and no mother or father, that Jimmy is make-believe. Mary Jane is fascinated by Ramona's very specific description of her "friend," but Eloise complains: "I get it all day long. Jimmy eats with her. Takes a bath with her. Sleeps with her. She sleeps way over on one side of the bed, so's not to roll over and hurt him." Eloise explains that because there are no children in the neighborhood, Ramona has managed to invent one herself. She sends Ramona outside again, and convinces Mary Jane to forget about her boss and have another drink.

Eloise mentions Walt, an old lover. She remembers him fondly because he made her laugh. Eloise tells Mary Jane about the time she was waiting for Walt at the bus stop. When the bus finally arrived, she was so excited that, in running to meet him, she fell and twisted her ankle. As Walt helped her up, he called her ankle "Poor Uncle Wiggily." Mary Jane asks if her husband Lew has a sense of humor, to which Eloise responds, "Oh, God! Who knows? Yes, I guess so. He laughs at cartoons and stuff." Mary Jane then says that humor is not everything in a relationship. Eloise recalls the time she and Walt were on a train together, just after he was drafted. She tells Mary Jane that she never told her husband about Walt because Lew would be interested only in Walt's rank in the service. Walt, according to Eloise, viewed rank differently from other soldiers: "He said that when he'd get his first promotion, instead of getting stripes he'd have his sleeves taken away from him. He said when he'd get to be general, he'd be stark naked. . . . Eloise looked over at Mary Jane, who wasn't laughing. Don't you think that's funny?" Eloise explains further that Lew is too unintelligent. She believes that women should tell men what they want to hear and should never give them credit for having any intelligence.

As their conversation continues, Mary Jane asks Eloise why she married her husband. She married him, she says, because Lew told her his favorite author was Jane Austen; it turned out that Lew had never read anything by Austen. Eloise thinks Mary Jane is better off because she has a job. Eloise insists she will never tell her husband about Walt because Walt is dead, in an accident that was the result of a selfish request his colonel made. Eloise is overcome by grief and begins to cry.

Ramona comes in again from outside. Eloise tries to get rid of the child, but Grace, the housekeeper, is busy. Eloise must contend with getting Ramona's boots off. Ramona announces that her friend Jimmy "got runned over and killed." Eloise asks Mary Jane to take her out to the kitchen to Grace and to bring back more drinks.

Time passes. The telephone rings. Mary Jane has passed out on the couch. Eloise answers the telephone in the dark. She tells her husband she won't be able to meet him because Mary Jane's car is blocking the driveway. She drinks the last of the Scotch and tells Grace to hold dinner. Because of the bad weather, Grace asks Eloise if her husband can stay overnight; Eloise says no. She then goes upstairs to look in on Ramona. She yells at her to wake her up. Ramona is sleeping on the left side of the bed to leave room for her new friend, Micky Mickeranno. She yells at her again, this time insisting that Ramona move to the center of the bed. Eloise turns off the light and bangs her leg as she crosses the room. She starts to cry and repeats to herself, "Poor Uncle Wiggily." Eloise bends over Ramona to tuck her in and sees that the child has been crying also. She kisses her and walks out.

ॐ

"The Laughing Man"

Before it was included in *Nine Stories*, this story appeared in *The New Yorker*, March 19, 1949.

When the narrator was nine years old, he belonged to the Comanche Club, a group of boys from his grammar school. Each day the boys were collected by their Chief, John Gedsudski, a twenty-two-year-old law student at New York University.

The Chief picked up the boys in front of P.S. 165 at three o'clock. On good days, he drove them in his converted bus to Central Park to play football, baseball, or other sports. If the weather was against them, the Chief took them on excursions to the Museum of Natural History or the Metropolitan Museum of Art. On Saturdays and holidays, John picked up the boys from each one's home and drove them all to the Palisades, for camping, or to Van Cortlandt Park, where there were regulation-size playing fields. These trips filled the boys' lives, but the part of the day they most enjoyed was the "Laughing Man," the weekly adventure story their Chief narrated to them when they returned to the bus at the end of an outing.

Chinese bandits had kidnapped the Laughing Man as a child and demanded a ransom from his missionary parents. When his parents refused to pay, the bandits tortured the boy, leaving him with a hairless, misshapen head and deformed facial features. His face was so ugly that he had to wear a mask made of poppy petals. The Laughing Man escaped to the forest, trailing behind him the scent of opium poppies. The forest animals befriended him, and soon he learned to speak their language. Among his animal friends, the Laughing Man wore no mask. The Laughing Man studied the criminal ways of the Chinese bandits and over time built his own business empire, outwitting the bandits at every turn. To conduct his affairs, the Laughing Man would often cross the China border into Paris, where his two dangerous enemies lived, Marcel Dufarge and his daughter. The Laughing Man amassed a great fortune, giving some of it away to charity and storing the rest as diamonds. He lived simply, eating only rice and drinking eagle's blood. Four loyal compatriots (Black Wing, Omba, Hong, and the beautiful girl) accompanied him regularly. The Laughing Man behaved formally with these devoted friends and always spoke to them through a black silk screen. By the time the Chief had related this much of the Laughing Man story, the nine-year-old narrator believed he was not his parents' child but instead a direct descendant of the Laughing Man, as did the other boys.

Now it is February. The Comanche Club is starting spring training for baseball season. The club's routine is broken by the appearance of a young woman, Mary Hudson. At first, the Chief hangs her picture by the driver's seat of the bus. The narrator remarks that this addition goes against the "men-only décor of the bus"; soon the picture becomes just another fixture. Then, after another installment of the "Laughing Man," Mary Hudson appears in person. The Chief is nervous with Mary present, and even worse, she insists on joining in on their baseball. The narrator, as captain of one of the teams, must accept her as a substitute center fielder. Despite the horror of all the boys and the uneasiness of the Chief, it turns out that Mary can hit quite well. A month or so passes and Mary gradually gains everyone's acceptance. The narrator comments fondly: "When you sat next to her on the bus, she smelled of a wonderful perfume."

One day in April, the Chief arrives unusually well dressed and neatly groomed when he picks up the boys. Instead of taking them to play, he parks the bus to wait for Mary and delivers another installment of the Laughing Man. In this episode, the Dufarges offer Black Wing's freedom in exchange for the Laughing Man. He agrees to this even though he knows how treacherous the Dufarges are. They have decided to substitute a fake Black Wing in order to capture the Laughing Man. Dufarge's daughter ties the Laughing Man to a tree with barbed wire. He speaks to the Black Wing imposter in timber wolf language and bids him farewell. The imposter listens to the Laughing Man for awhile, confesses that he is a fake, and then flees China. While this is happening the Laughing Man manages to knock off his mask. When Mlle. Dufarge sees his face, she faints. Her father manages to cover his eyes. The installment and the waiting for Mary end.

The Comanche Club boys drive off to their ball game. The narrator later sees Mary in the stands and points her out to the Chief. Both Mary and the Chief are behaving oddly. The narrator asks Mary to join in the game, but she snaps at him and runs off crying. This is the last time that the Chief and Mary are together. When the narrator questions him, the Chief changes the subject: "I went over to him and asked if he and Mary Hudson had had a fight. He told me to tuck my shirt in." When the boys return to the bus, the Chief upbraids them. They sit perfectly still as the Chief begins what turns out to be the last installment of the Laughing Man, which takes only five minutes to recount.

Dufarge's bullets have struck the Laughing Man, two of them in the heart. Because Dufarge and his daughter think he is dying, they try to see what his face looks like with his mask off. But the Laughing Man is not dead. As the Dufarges approach him, the Laughing Man vomits all four bullets. At this, the Dufarges drop dead. The Laughing Man is still tied to the tree with barbed wire. Several days pass. The Laughing Man is dying a slow death, and the Dufarges' bodies are decaying at his feet. He calls to the animals to get his friend Omba. By the time Omba arrives, the Laughing Man is in a coma. Omba puts back his mask, dresses his wounds, and offers him some eagle's blood to drink. The Laughing Man asks about Black Wing. Omba tells him that the Dufarges have killed his beloved Black Wing. The Laughing Man refuses the blood and tells Omba to look away as he removes his mask. Then he dies.

One of the Comanche boys bursts into tears. All of the boys are shaken by this sad ending. Arriving at his house, the narrator sees some red tissue paper on a lamppost. When he enters his home, he is shaking so badly he is sent to bed.

∾

"For Esmé—with Love and Squalor"

The last of the war-themed short stories, this one appeared in *The New Yorker* on April 8, 1950 before being published as part of *Nine Stories*. Like "A Perfect Day for Bananafish," it has been the subject of much critical analysis.

The story is actually two separate but overlapping stories. The narrator begins by stating that he has received an invitation to attend Esmé's wedding, to take place in England. He cannot attend, however, since he has promised his wife they would visit her mother. The narrator then proceeds to describe Esmé, whom he met six years earlier.

In April 1944, the narrator is one of sixty American soldiers involved in pre-Invasion training in Devon, England. The men do not socialize, preferring instead to write letters or read: "Rainy days, I generally sat in a dry place and read a book, often just an axe length away from a Ping-Pong table."

At the end of the training course, the narrator packs his belongings, puts some books in his gas mask bag (having thrown away the mask sometime earlier), and although it was raining heavily, dresses, goes outside, and walks through the lightning toward town.

Eventually he comes to a church, where he stops to read the bulletin board. The choir is in practice. The narrator enters the church and sees some adults and many boots lined up in a row. About twenty children, mostly girls ages seven to thirteen, are seated in rows on the rostrum. Their choir leader is shouting at them to open their beaks like little dickeybirds. The narrator thinks their singing is melodious but notes that one girl stands out from the rest. She is about thirteen years old, with ash-blond hair and "blasé eyes." Her voice is better than the others', but she seems bored.

The narrator leaves the church when the children finish their practice. Although it is still raining, the narrator continues his walk. He decides against the Red Cross recreation station and goes instead to the civilian tearoom. He finds a place to sit and read two letters from home.

The girl from the choir practice, wet from the storm, enters with her younger brother and their governess. When their tea arrives, she sees the narrator is staring at her. She smiles at him. She walks over to his table and sits down. She proceeds to comment on tea and Americans in general. She introduces herself as Esmé and tells him that she noticed him at choir practice.

When the narrator praises her voice, Esmé tells him of her plans. She intends to become a professional, to sing jazz on the radio, to make money, and to live on a ranch in Ohio. Then Esmé tells him that he is the eleventh American she has met. She chatters on about Americans and her opinions of them. She talks about her hair and then asks the narrator if he loves his wife; she thinks he is lonely. She explains that she has lived with her aunt since her mother died. She does not give her full name or her title.

Charles, Esmé's young brother, interrupts them to sit down at the table. Esmé introduces him to the narrator and remarks that her brother is quite brilliant. Esmé says, in front of her brother, that their father was "s-l-a-i-n" in North Africa. Charles then turns to the narrator and gives him the Bronx cheer. Charles asks the narrator a riddle and then shouts out the answer. Esmé continues their conversation and asks about the narrator's profession. When he tells her that he is a writer, she remarks that her father wrote brilliantly and shows him her father's wristwatch. Then she asks him to write a short story about her someday. "'It doesn't have to be terribly prolific! Just so that it isn't childish and silly.' She reflected. 'I prefer stories about squalor. . . . I'm extremely interested in squalor.'"

Charles asks the riddle again. This time the narrator delivers the punch line, which makes the boy react furiously. Esmé says that their mother spoiled him. As she excuses herself from the table, she informs the narrator that they come to the tearoom every Saturday after choir practice. She asks if he would enjoy receiving letters from her. He gives her his address and waves as they leave. The boy returns to say that he wants a kiss goodbye, although he seems to have been obligated to do this by his sister. This time the narrator asks Charles the riddle, which makes the boy light up. Esmé reminds the narrator of his promise to write a story and bids goodbye, saying, "I hope you return from the war with all your faculties intact."

In what appears to be a second story, the tone shifts. "This is the squalid, or moving, part of the story, and the scene changes. . . . I'm still around, but from here on in, for reasons I'm not at liberty to disclose, I've disguised myself so cunningly that even the cleverest reader will fail to recognize me." The narrator is now Staff Sergeant X. It is weeks after V-E Day. He is in a house in Bavaria that belonged to the daughter of a Nazi. He and nine other soldiers are living there now. X has been reading a book with considerable difficulty. Not all his faculties are intact, and he finds himself rereading the same passage several times.

Putting the book down, he lights another cigarette. He has been chain-smoking for some time. Then he stops and feels "his mind dislodge itself and teeter, like insecure luggage on an overhead rack." On the table in front of X are unopened letters and packages addressed to him. He picks up a book by Goebbels that belonged to the homeowner's daughter. He remembers that he arrested her because of her Nazi connections. Inside he reads the inscription: "Dear God, life is hell." He adds to the inscription a quote from Dostoyevsky: "Fathers and teachers, I ponder 'What is hell?' I maintain that it is the suffering of being unable to love." When he finishes writing, he sees that what he wrote is illegible. He drops the book and picks up an old letter from his brother. In it his brother asks him to bring home some war souvenirs, like bayonets or swastikas. He puts his head down to rest on the table. "He was rather like a Christmas tree whose lights, wired in series, must all go out if even one bulb is defective."

Just then, Clay, who is Corporal Z, enters the room. Clay is large and well dressed. He and X have been through many campaigns together in the war. Clay remarks that X's hands are shaking. He asks how much weight X lost while in the hospital. X changes the subject and asks about Loretta, Clay's girlfriend. X knows all about Loretta because Clay read him all her letters, even the intimate ones, and then asked X to write the replies.

Clay sees a nervous tic in X's face, which X attempts to cover with his hand. Clay says that he has told Loretta all about X's problems because she majors in psychology at college. "You know what she said? She says nobody gets a nervous breakdown just from the war and all. She says you probably were unstable like, your whole goddam life." Then Clay reminds him of the cat Clay shot at after they had been shelled for two hours. Clay told this to Loretta in a letter that she then brought to class so that the professor and her classmates could analyze it. Loretta wrote Clay back that he shot at the cat because he was temporarily insane. But X disagrees: "You weren't insane. You were simply doing your duty. You killed that pussycat in as manly a way as anybody." Clay reacts harshly to these remarks. Then X turns his head away and vomits. Clay tries to convince X to join him for the radio show, but X declines. Clay suggests that X rest and then leaves.

X stares at his portable typewriter, thinking it would do him good to write to an old friend in New York. He closes his eyes to rest from the pain. When he opens them, he sees a package and opens it. It contains a letter and something wrapped in tissue paper. In her usual, precise wording, Esmé apologizes for letting thirty-eight days pass before writing to him. In the same grown-up tone she used with him before, Esmé writes about D-Day and her brother. In the postscript, she tells X she is enclosing her father's wristwatch, which she hopes he will accept as "a lucky talisman." Some time passes before X can take the wristwatch out of the package. When he does, he notices that the crystal is broken. He sits and stares at the watch and finally falls asleep. As the story closes, X feels that he has "a chance of again becoming a man with all his fac—with all his f-a-c-u-l-t-i-e-s intact."

∾

"Franny"

"Franny" was first published in *The New Yorker* on January 29, 1955; it was later released in book form, along with "Zooey," in 1961, by Little, Brown. Salinger continues his exposition and development of the Glass family, specifically of Franny, their youngest child.

As the story opens, twenty young men are waiting at a train station for their dates to arrive for the Yale game weekend. They cluster in small groups and sound "collegiately dogmatic, as though each young man, in his strident, conversational turn, was clearing up, once and for all, some highly controversial issue, one that the outside, non-matriculating world had been bungling, provocatively or not, for centuries."

Lane Coutell, standing slightly away from the others, waits inside and rereads a much-handled letter. It has been written, that is typewritten, by Franny Glass, the young woman whose arrival Lane is anticipating. In the letter, she writes of looking forward to the weekend, of loving Lane to "distraction," and of looking "down on all poets except Sappho."

A young man interrupts Lane's reading to ask if he understands the poet Rilke; Lane tolerates his presence only until the train arrives. Lane spots Franny at the far end of the platform and waves at her enthusiastically. Walking toward her, Lane sees her raccoon coat and remembers fondly once kissing Franny and then the coat as if it were an extension of her.

They greet each other warmly. Franny does most of the talking—about girls she knew on the train, about the Smith types, along with the "types" from Vassar, Bennington, and Sarah Lawrence. Lane apologizes for not getting her better accommodations. They drop off her bags and then go to Strickler's, a popular restaurant. After martinis, Lane shows his satisfaction at being in the right place at the right time—and with the "right-looking girl." Franny can see how pleased Lane is with himself, "but by some old, standing arrangement with her psyche, she elected to feel guilty for having seen it, caught it, and sentenced herself to listen to Lane's ensuing conversation with a special semblance of absorption."

Lane talks at length about a paper he has written. Franny interrupts, asking for his martini olive. Lane begins again, adding this time that he was told he should publish his paper. Franny accuses him of sounding like a "section man," someone who stands in during a professor's absence. "He's usually a graduate student or something. Anyway, if it's a course in Russian Literature, say, he comes in, in his little button-down-collar shirt and striped tie, and starts knocking Turgenev for about a half hour. Then, when he's finished, when he's completely ruined Turgenev for you, he starts talking about Stendhal or somebody he wrote his thesis for his M.A. on."

Lane takes offense and Franny apologizes. She explains that she has felt very destructive lately. She seems easily distracted and apologizes again. They continue talking about college. They order more martinis. Franny complains about the English department and school in general. "It's just that if I had any guts at all, I wouldn't have gone back to college at all this year. I don't know. I mean it's all the most incredible farce." When Lane insists that she is lucky to have two real poets in her English department, Franny strongly disagrees with him and asks to change the subject. She excuses herself again, explaining that she is not feeling well. Then she goes on. "If you're a poet, you do something beautiful. I mean you're supposed to leave something beautiful after you get off the page and everything. The ones you're talking about don't leave a single, solitary thing beautiful." Lane isn't paying attention and is surprised when Franny leaves for the ladies' room. His earlier contentment has disappeared. The raccoon coat that had evoked pleasant memories earlier now annoys him. Seeing a classmate enter with a date, Lane adjusts himself at the table so that he looks "bored, preferably attractively bored."

The ladies' room is empty. Franny enters the farthest stall and locks the door behind her. She sits down and presses her hands over her eyes. Then she breaks down and cries. Composed once more, she reaches for her purse and pulls out a small book. She looks at it and holds it to her chest. Without opening it, she puts it back in her handbag.

When Franny returns to the table, Lane orders dinner, even though Franny told him she isn't hungry. Lane asks the waiter to bring her a chicken sandwich and then orders snails and frogs' legs for himself. Their conversation continues to be strained. Lane talks about their weekend plans, which include meeting his friend Wally Campbell. Franny reacts badly again and complains about the Wally Campbells of their class who are charming, who gossip, and who invariably spend the summer in Italy. Lane tells her that she looks pale and that she should eat, but Franny asks him to eat without her. When he asks how her play has been going, she informs him that she has quit because she cannot tolerate being around so much ego. Lane is confused, since the theater has been a favorite topic of Franny's. When he accuses her of being afraid to compete, Franny insists that she quit precisely because she was afraid she would compete. When she takes a handkerchief from her purse, she puts her little book on the table.

Franny jumps when Lane asks about the book. She says it is called "The Way of a Pilgrim" and makes little of it. She explains that an anonymous Russian peasant wrote it and that it explains the pilgrim's quest to understand how to pray incessantly. She now monopolizes the conversation while he enjoys his frogs' legs. Franny explains the pilgrim's philosophy but Lane pays more attention to the food. Franny continues her explication of the text and its relation to the "Philokalia," another book on mystical thought. She says that the pilgrim learned that if you say the Jesus Prayer repeatedly, it becomes active. "Something happens after a while. I don't know what, but something happens, and the words get synchronized with the person's heartbeats . . . which has a really tremendous, mystical effect on your whole outlook." Lane is not paying attention; finally, he asks if Franny really believes all this "mumbo-jumbo." He says she is ignoring the place that psychology holds in any discussion of religious experience. Franny interrupts to leave the table again because she feels "funny." As she walks past the bar, she faints and collapses on the floor.

As the story ends, Lane is sitting beside Franny when she regains consciousness. He now focuses completely on her. Lane tells her that rest is more important than their weekend plans, especially since they haven't had any time together for over a month. As he leaves her to get some water, "her lips began to move, forming soundless words, and they continued to move."

ॐ

"Raise High the Roof Beam, Carpenters"

Before being published with "Seymour: An Introduction" in book form in 1963 by Little, Brown, "Raise High the Roof Beam, Carpenters" appeared in *The New Yorker* on November 19, 1955. The story is about Seymour Glass, six years before the time "A Perfect Day for Bananafish" takes place.

Buddy Glass, second of the seven Glass children, narrates the events surrounding Seymour's marriage to Muriel. Buddy sets the stage by explaining how he has become the designated attendee at the wedding. It is May 1942. The two youngest Glass children, Franny and Zooey, accompanied by their parents, are in Los Angeles as guests on the radio show "It's a Wise Child." The twins, Walt and Waker, are also away: Waker in a conscientious objectors' camp, and Walt somewhere in action in the Pacific. The oldest girl, Boo Boo, is in the Waves, stationed in Brooklyn. In a letter Buddy includes as part of his narration, Boo Boo has named Buddy the obligated wedding-goer. Shortly after he receives the letter, Buddy is released from an Army hospital, where he was recuperating from pleurisy. A few days later he finds himself, his ribs wrapped in adhesive tape, surrounded by people he doesn't know, all waiting for a wedding to begin.

The next part of the story concentrates on the uncomfortable situation in which Buddy finds himself: after two hours, the groom has still not appeared. After the bride has been driven off in one of the hired limousines, the rest of the guests (members of the bride's immediate family), are invited to use the rest of the limousines to return to the bride's parents' apartment. Buddy is helping people into the waiting cars. Soon he is in one of the cars himself, with four other people: Mrs. Helen Silsburn; the Matron of Honor, "a hefty girl of about twenty-four or -five, in a pink satin dress, with a circlet of artificial forget-me-nots in her hair"; her husband; and an elderly man in top hat and cutaway. When Mrs. Silsburn asks if Buddy is a friend of the bride or the groom, the Matron of Honor interrupts: "You'd better not say you're a friend of the groom. . . . I'd like to get my hands on him for about two minutes. Just two minutes, that's all." Her husband, a Lieutenant dressed in his Signal Corps uniform, chuckles loudly. The Matron of Honor continues her harangue against the missing groom. She and Mrs. Silsburn compare notes and agree that nobody has met the groom and they know little about him. The Matron of Honor is aware, however, that Seymour had telephoned Muriel, the forsaken bride, very late from some hotel so that they could talk.

Buddy jumps into the conversation to ask the name of the hotel. He admits to knowing Seymour, but only when "we were boys together," a comment that provokes further wrath from the Matron of Honor. As they grill Buddy about Seymour, he suffers a coughing fit. His reprieve from questioning is only temporary. When they ask Seymour's profession, Buddy says, "He's a chiropodist." At this point they notice that the car is stopped in traffic because of a parade.

The Matron of Honor and Mrs. Silsburn are particularly upset because they want to be with Muriel to comfort her. They ask the driver to check with the police on duty. He complies, but is of no help when he returns to the car. While they wait, they offer cigarettes all around and complain of the cramped quarters. The Matron of Honor and Mrs. Silsburn begin to piece together all the information relating to the wedding. They consider Muriel's mother brilliant but discreet for not opposing the marriage. As Muriel's mother has said that Seymour was "a really schizoid personality," both women conclude that Muriel is actually better off not to have married him. Buddy can contain himself no longer. "What brought Mrs. Fedder to the conclusion that Seymour is a latent homosexual and a schizoid personality?" The Matron of Honor asks him if he thinks a normal man would spend the night talking to his fiancée to explain that he is too happy to get married. Buddy questions her again. While she is answering him, she interrupts herself: "Do you know who I think you are? I think you're this Seymour's brother." Buddy admits the truth.

His confession refuels her attacks on Seymour and his family. She accuses Buddy of being one of the children on "It's a Wise Child." The lieutenant tries to calm her. She declares that she has always hated the radio show and is about to continue when the sounds of an approaching marching band interrupt her. She suggests that they abandon the car to look for a telephone. On leaving the car, the Matron of Honor invites Buddy to join them. As they all leave, in trying to wake the elderly man, they realize he is a deaf-mute. They walk down the street in search of a telephone but have no luck. Buddy tells them that his apartment is close by. He invites them to stop there to use the telephone and to rest. The Matron of Honor hesitates and then asks if Seymour will be there. Buddy thinks not.

The Matron of Honor says, "And all I have to say is he'd better not be there when we get there, or I'll kill the bastard."

The tempers that have flared so far begin to subside as the five of them enter Buddy's apartment. Buddy walks in ahead of them to make sure that Seymour indeed is not present. He offers to make them all cool drinks and tries to turn on the air conditioner. The Matron of Honor continues her tirade about Seymour and relates more details provided by Mrs. Fedder. Buddy can contain himself no longer. "I said I didn't give a good God damn what Mrs. Fedder had to say on the subject of Seymour. Or, for that matter, what any professional dilettante or amateur bitch had to say." He tells them how brilliant Seymour is and what wonderful poems he writes. When he finishes, Buddy's heart is racing.

The Matron of Honor asks to use the telephone. When Buddy shows her the bedroom where the telephone is, he sees Seymour's diary. He grabs it, tucks it under his arm, and stands in the hall for a moment to consider what to do with it.

Buddy suspends the narration here to insert several pages from Seymour's diary, in which Seymour is reminiscing about the radio show "It's a Wise Child" and remembering being grilled by Mrs. Fedder's analyst. He writes how he felt obligated to Muriel to go to a psychoanalyst. "Oh, God, if I'm anything by a clinical name, I'm a kind of paranoiac in reverse. I suspect people of plotting to make me happy." Buddy closes the diary and goes to the kitchen to make the drinks. He pours himself a Scotch, thinking that "this was . . . no ordinary day."

When Buddy returns to the living room, he begins telling his guests anecdotes from the Glass children's days on "It's a Wise Child," including the time Seymour hit a child so hard she needed stitches. At this, the guests discover that the Matron of Honor was that obnoxious child.

The Matron of Honor returns from her telephone call, her mood much improved. Seymour and Muriel have eloped and Mrs. Fedder sounded "absolutely normal." Making their goodbyes, the guests leave for Mrs. Fedder's apartment. Buddy is now beginning to feel the effects of the Scotch and the stress of the day. In the bathroom, Buddy reads the last entry in Seymour's diary: "I've been reading a miscellany of Vedanta all day. Marriage partners are to serve each other. Elevate, help, teach, strengthen each other, but above all, serve. Raise their children honorably." Buddy returns to the bedroom and collapses on the bed. An hour and a half later, he wakes up quite thirsty. In the living room, he realizes that his last guest has left. Buddy observes, "Only his empty glass, and his cigar end in the pewter ashtray, indicated that he had ever existed." ❁

List of Characters

"A Perfect Day for Bananafish"

Muriel Glass, married to Seymour Glass, is accustomed to the good things in life. She feigns boredom on the telephone when her mother repeatedly expresses concern over Seymour. Muriel seems more interested in a vacation in Florida than in her husband's mental health.

Muriel's mother is a concerned, perhaps overanxious, woman who worries that her daughter may come to some harm at the hands of her son-in-law, Seymour. She counsels Muriel to pay attention to the psychiatrist's warning. She also suggests that Muriel accept money from her father to take a vacation without her husband.

Mrs. Carpenter is a guest at the same hotel where Seymour and Muriel are staying. She seems more willing to have a martini with her friend than to watch over her daughter, Sybil.

Sybil Carpenter, the four-year-old girl who calls her beach companion "See more glass." She plays and talks with Seymour. Seymour tells her the story of the bananafish.

ॐ

"Uncle Wiggily in Connecticut"

Mary Jane is Eloise's friend from college. They both left school before graduating because of the men in their lives. Mary Jane is now a career woman who visits Eloise at her home in the country.

Eloise is an unhappy, suburban housewife. Eloise is married to Lew but remembers her lover, Walt, with fondness. She fills her days with drink and gossip. Eloise impatiently tends to her young daughter, whom she treats with the same tediousness as her husband.

Ramona, Eloise's young and very imaginative daughter, wears thick glasses and creates imaginary friends.

Lew Wengler is Eloise's husband. Eloise talks about him to Mary Jane and to him over the telephone.

Walt is Eloise's former lover, killed in the Second World War in a freak accident. Eloise remembers him most for his sense of humor, something that she feels her husband lacks.

Grace, Eloise's housekeeper, serves to keep Ramona out of her mother's way. When Grace is busy, Eloise is forced to deal with Ramona herself.

&

"The Laughing Man"

John Gedsudski, known as the Chief, is a twenty-two-year-old law student at New York University. In an arrangement with their parents, he chaperones a group of grammar-school boys to the park each day for sports and camping. The Chief tells the boys the story of the Laughing Man, which he delivers in regular installments.

The narrator (as a nine-year-old boy) is a member of the Comanche Club, captain of their baseball team, and, like the other boys in the club, impressed by the exploits of the Laughing Man.

Mary Hudson, John's girlfriend, attends Wellesley College, a "high-class" school, according to John, which implies that she comes from a wealthier family than he does. Mary invites herself into the formerly male-only Comanche Club and plays baseball with them. Mary and John have a falling-out, which takes its toll on the boys.

The Laughing Man is the character the Chief has created to entertain the boys after their games. John provides new installments only if the boys behave well. The Laughing Man is a heroic character who outwits his enemies and protects his friends. He wears a mask made of poppy petals to conceal his deformed face, the result of torture by Chinese bandits when he was a boy.

The four loyal to Laughing Man:
Black Wing, a timber wolf: The Dufarges use Black Wing as a ploy to capture the Laughing Man.

Omba, a dwarf: Omba brings the Laughing Man eagle's blood to try to save his life.

Hong, a Mongolian giant.

A Eurasian girl.

Marcel Dufarge and his daughter, Mlle. Dufarge: These are the Laughing Man's archenemies. They regularly conspire against him.

❧

"For Esmé—with Love and Squalor"

Esmé is a thirteen-year-old English girl who has lost both her parents in the war. Her younger brother Charles and their governess, Miss Megley, accompany her to tea. Esmé speaks and acts much older than her years imply. She offers the narrator her many opinions on Americans, the war, and life. She sends him her dead father's wristwatch to bring him luck.

Mother Grencher, the mother-in-law of the narrator, whose impending visit prevents him from attending Esmé's wedding.

Charles is the five-year-old brother of Esmé, who enjoys shocking adults and telling riddles.

Sergeant X, the narrator's alter ego in the second and "squalid" part of the story, is recuperating after "losing his faculties because of the war." He chain-smokes and has difficulty concentrating when he reads. He suffers from painful headaches but still manages to write letters for Clay.

Clay (Corporal Z) has been at the narrator's side through many campaigns of the war but does not show the strain the narrator shows. He is a gregarious sort who plans to marry his girlfriend, Loretta, after the war.

Loretta, Clay's girlfriend, shares his letters about the war with the professor and classmates in her psychology class. She does not believe that the narrator has suffered a nervous breakdown and has reached the opinion that he probably had something wrong with him before the war.

❧

"Franny"

Franny is the youngest child in the Glass family. She appears in several of Salinger's works. As the youngest, she carries the weight of the older children's talents and faults. She has arrived to spend the weekend with her boyfriend, who attends Yale.

Lane Coutell is Franny's boyfriend. He anticipates a wonderful weekend with Franny. As they dine, Lane reluctantly listens to Franny's analysis of mystical thought and The Pilgrim's Prayer. Lane would rather think about the frogs' legs and snails he has ordered for dinner and would rather discuss the upcoming events of the weekend.

ow

"Raise High the Roof Beam, Carpenters"

Buddy Glass, a young soldier, is the narrator of the story and the brother of its central character, Seymour. Because Seymour has disappeared on his wedding day, Buddy finds himself in a rather awkward situation in a hot and crowded New York City limousine. He has only recently left an Army hospital, having been treated for pleurisy. He is forced to defend his brother to a group of strangers.

Seymour Glass is the older brother of the narrator, Buddy. It is his wedding day.

Mrs. Helen Silsburn, a well-dressed woman of about fifty, rides in the limousine with Buddy and some of the bride's guests.

The Matron of Honor, Mrs. Burwick: A hefty twenty-four-year-old woman. She is angry at Seymour for standing up Muriel at their wedding.

Her husband, the Lieutenant, in his Signal Corps uniform, tries to calm the other passengers in the limousine. He is proud of his vocal wife but shows some concern for Buddy's health.

The elderly man, the last passenger in the limousine, neither speaks nor pays attention. For Buddy, the little man is a reassuring presence.

Muriel Fedder Glass is the bride-to-be.

Mrs. Fedder, Muriel's mother, doesn't take part in the action but in her absence she weighs heavily on Buddy. She is thought discreet by Mrs. Silsburn and the Matron of Honor but has provided them with details about Seymour, his past, and his odd behavior. ❀

Critical Views on
J. D. Salinger

PETER BUITENHUIS ON THE FICTION OF J. D. SALINGER

[Peter Buitenhuis questions why Salinger was so unproductive a writer and yet, like Esmé, so interested in squalor. Buitenhuis maintains that Salinger's only concern is that of Albert Camus's, in the *Myth of Sisyphus:* whether man should commit suicide.]

Why Salinger should have become so relatively unproductive is a more difficult question and one, clearly, that has been a major concern of Salinger himself from near the beginning of his career. In one of the *Nine Stories,* "For Esmé with Love and Squalor" Esmé asks the narrator of the story—someone who appears to be very closely identified with Salinger himself—to write a story exclusively for herself:

> I told her I certainly would, if I could. I said that I wasn't terribly prolific.
> "It doesn't have to be so terribly prolific! Just so that it isn't childish and silly." She reflected. "I prefer stories about squalor."
> "About what?" I said, leaning forward.
> "Squalor. I'm extremely interested in squalor."

Salinger is extremely interested in squalor too. In fact most, if not all, of his fiction is about the subject, in one form or another. The first of the *Nine Stories,* "A Perfect Day for Banana Fish" is about a figure who is to haunt all of Salinger's fiction, Seymour Glass. He is on holiday in Florida with his wife after the Second World War. His wife reports to her mother on the telephone to New York that Seymour has called her "Miss Spiritual Tramp of 1948." Seymour, who spends most of the story playing with a little girl on the beach, returns to the hotel room at the end of the story. He finds his wife napping on her bed. He takes an Ortgies calibre 7.65 automatic from his suitcase, sits on the unoccupied bed, aims the pistol, and puts a bullet through his right temple.

Seymour Glass's decision is, I believe, a central clue to the fact that Salinger is not prolific. He would agree with Albert Camus in *The Myth of Sisyphus* that the only serious philosophical question a man has to face is whether or not to commit suicide. From the tension and agony of spirit that the reader can feel lying behind all of Salinger's fiction, we can feel that he has considered this way out many times too. More affirmative answers, I believe, have only been reached through the hard-won triumphs of his art. More recently, there have been indications that his affirmations have been made in the form of mystical experience.

Some of the *Nine Stories* and all of the subsequent fiction seem to represent at least partly achieved solutions to spiritual problems. As such they seem to have taken their toll of his artistic, if not his spiritual, capital. His more recent fiction, unhappily, tends to resolve itself into religious, rather than dramatic terms. It seems to be the product of an intense contemplation that has been projected into the minds of his highly articulate characters, but not sufficiently into their lives.

—Peter Buitenhuis, "The Sound of One Hand Clapping: the Fiction of J. D. Salinger," *Five American Moderns* (Toronto: Roger Ascham Press, 1968), pp. 36–38

IAN HAMILTON ON THE SEARCH FOR J. D. SALINGER

[Ian Hamilton's unauthorized book about Salinger's life prompted Salinger to bring litigation against both Hamilton and his publisher, Random House. Because the biography was finally published, albeit in a different form, Hamilton felt he had, in the end, won the lawsuit. In this excerpt, Hamilton describes receiving, after many requests, his first response from Salinger.]

About three weeks after the first wave of answers had subsided, I got a letter from J. D. Salinger himself. One of *my* letters, it seems, had been received by his sister, and another by his son—both of whom are listed in the Manhattan phone book. Salinger berated me for harassing his family "in the not particularly fair name of scholarship." He didn't suppose he could stop me writing a book about him, but he thought he ought to let me know—"for whatever little it may be worth"—that he had suffered so many intrusions on his privacy that he could endure no more of it—not "in a single lifetime."

The letter was touching in a way, but also just a shade repellent. It was as frigidly impersonal as it could be, and somewhat too composed, too pleased with its own polish for me to accept it as a direct cry from the heart. And yet there could be no mistaking its intent. I tried it out on one or two of my more sardonic literary friends. One said that it was "really a kind of come-on": "I can't stop you" to be translated as "Please go ahead." Another said: "Who does he think he is?" and I suppose this was closer to my own response. But it was hard for me to be certain what I felt. I has already accepted a commission for this book. I'd been paid (and I'd already spent) a fair amount of money. According to my original plan (that Salinger might perhaps be lured into the open), it could be said that things were working out quite well. And yet this human contact, icy though it was, did give me pause. Up to now, I'd been dallying with the idea of Salinger; he was a fictional character, almost, and certainly a symbolic one, in the fable of American letters. He said he wanted neither fame nor money and by this means he'd contrived to get extra supplies of both—much more of both, in fact, than might have come his way if he'd stayed in the marketplace along with everybody else. Surely, I'd been reasoning in my more solemn moments, there was some lesson to be learned from his "career." To what extent was Salinger the victim of America's cultural star system? To what extent its finest flower? American intellectuals look with compassion on those Eastern bloc writers who have been silenced by the state, but here, in their own culture, a greatly loved author had elected to silence himself. He had freedom of speech but what he had ended up wanting more than anything else, it seemed, was the freedom to be silent. And the power to silence—to silence anyone who wanted to find out why he had stopped speaking.

And yet here was this letter, obliging me to face up to the presence of the man himself. He wanted to be left alone. He'd kept his side of the bargain: by not publishing, by refusing all interviews, photographs, and so on. He hadn't gone quite so far as to withdraw his books from circulation, but perhaps it wasn't in his power to do so. He had, it would appear, behaved with dignity and forbearance whenever some eager college student had turned up at his door.

Didn't he have the same right to his privacy as you and I? Well, yes.
But then again, not quite.

—Ian Hamilton, *In Search of J. D. Salinger* (New York: Random
House, 1988), pp. 7–8

HELEN WEINBERG ON HOLDEN AND SEYMOUR AND THE SPIRITUAL ACTIVIST HERO

[Weinberg warns against "facile Freudian criticism"
regarding Salinger's work. She explains that Salinger's character development often falls both outside normal and
abnormal behavior and examines the characters of Seymour Glass and Holden Caulfield to demonstrate the
behavioral differences between the two.]

Facile Freudian criticism of modern literature is no longer possible.
Perhaps Freud's insights clarify great literary intuitions of the past.
We may realize Hamlet's situation to a fuller extent if Hamlet is seen
in the light of the Oedipal complex. However, today's literature is
post-Freudian: it starts from Freud; it includes Freud; it leaps out of
and away from Freud; it opposes itself to Freudian clichés along with
a host of other sorts of inherited clichés. The post-Freudian novelist
has been given what the post-Freudian critic or reader has been
given. I think a modern novelist expects the reader to assume the
Freudian ideas with him as part of the general intelligence which he
brings to bear on (or which he opposes to) the reality that he presents in his novel.

It is, in fact, on the basis of the recognition that the investigation
of heroes with wonderfully varied psyches and an assortment of psychological differences which remain outside Freudian (or other
established psychological) categories is possible in literature that I
would find fault with much of the favorable and unfavorable criticism of Salinger. Salinger, as many new novelists do, explores possi-
bilities outside normal behavior and outside the usual categories for
abnormal behavior. Clearly, today's novelists are not psychological
realists in any of the established ways.

However, Salinger may attract critiques based on psychological categorizing from his admirers and detractors because he cheats, especially in his earlier work, on his own vision (a vision of goodness on the edge of madness) in order to structure a story according to external, formalized rules of the storytelling craft. I am not talking of the twenty stories of the apprentice period; these are experiments in storytelling in a number of styles: the styles of F. Scott Fitzgerald, Katherine Mansfield, and a little of the simple surprise-ending stuff of O. Henry. Nor do I find a conflict between vision and form in seven of the *Nine Stories*. All except "Teddy" and "De Daumier-Smith's Blue Period" are formal studies of love and loneliness; all have *The New Yorker* tone as they make their understatements on the sweet and the sad in modern life. They are, no matter how successful of their kind (in the way, for example, that "For Esmé with Love and Squalor" is successful), slight and ephemeral. They are informed by no special vision.

—Helen Weinberg, "J. D. Salinger's Holden and Seymour and the Spiritual Activist Hero," *The New Novel in America* (Ithaca, NY: Cornell University Press, 1970), pp. 142–43

John Russell on Salinger's Feat

[The author of the prize-winning *Henry Green*, John Russell discusses Salinger's use of foot imagery. He lists some examples of "leg-crossers," explains Seymour Glass's foot fetish, and examines the relationships between feet and Buddhist thought.]

With unusualness, or unusual repetitiveness, being the criterion for admitting Salinger's feet to discussion, I now ask for latitude—for the indulgence of admitting examples from the thighs down. More can be done this way toward making Salinger's meanings bulk more solid. Uncle Wiggily up there in Connecticut, for example, is an ankle. Feet, ankles, shins, knees, thighs—let these be enough of dem bones for us to try to connect up into something.

Let us start with a look at the leg-crossers in *Nine Stories*. Does a rather insistent undertone develop—Salinger is always quiet in these early stories—when

(a) Muriel Glass is shown crossing her legs three times, during a telephone conversation in which she coolly assures her mother that she can handle her husband Seymour—then only minutes away from suicide;

(b) Eloise Wengler is "stretched out on the couch, her thin but very pretty legs crossed at the ankles," preparatory to a scene with a friend in which she languidly reveals her resentment of her daughter Ramona and her open contempt for her husband Lew;

(c) Ginnie Mannox, in a belligerent mood and determined to give a young man she's never met, Franklin Graff, the coolest possible greeting, "crossed her long legs, arranged the hem of her polo coat over her knees, and waited";

(d) Mary Hudson, having got through the interview at the Comanches' ball game in which she has cut John Gedsudski adrift from her, sits on a players' bench, lights a cigarette, and crosses her legs; and

(e) Bob Nicholson, half-skeptical, half-nosy, entirely patronizing toward Teddy McArdle during their sundeck conversation, is described as crossing his "heavy legs, at the ankles," twice?

Or should I have asked first: Is it not illuminating that Salinger repeats these descriptions? If an undertone of some strength does develop, I think it grows out of this factor common to all five instances: that the four young women and the young man are all self-possessed. Typical of Salinger characters who at such moments have nothing to offer anybody, they are consciously composed, smug really (except Mary Hudson), assured of the upper hand in what may be verbal exchanges but where the human stakes are considerable.

People with their legs crossed are observable everywhere, of course, but Salinger selects this position, the controlled poise of it, to heighten situations that lead nowhere in terms of human giving, and everywhere in terms of a character's keeping one jump ahead of experience. These characters are unexposed (in contrast, Uncle Wiggily got its endearing name when it was a twisted ankle); being so self-contained, they are unable to supply the needs of others: Muriel can't supply Seymour's, Eloise can't supply Ramona's, Ginnie can't supply Franklin's, Mary Hudson can't supply the Laughing Man's.

—John Russell, "Salinger's Feat," *Modern Fiction Studies* 12, no. 3 (Autumn 1966): 300–301

Critical Views on
"A Perfect Day for Bananafish"

BARBARA KORTE ON NARRATIVE PERSPECTIVE IN THE WORKS OF J. D. SALINGER

[Unlike most Salinger critics who have concentrated on thematic interpretations, Barbara Korte examines the narrative technique at play in Salinger's stories. She maintains that Salinger's use of "external focalization" develops a sense of immediacy, which makes the reader feel he is a "direct witness to the scene."]

The bulk of scholarly attention to Salinger has been devoted to his themes. The influence of Eastern mysticism and Western existentialism, the role of aberrant psychology or the figure of the outsider are frequent topics of comment. His narrative technique, on the other hand, has been little studied. Yet Salinger's handling of point of view often contravenes prevailing norms of modern fiction and is therefore of particular interest.

Salinger's best-known short stories, in contrast to *The Catcher in the Rye,* furnish some near-perfect examples of one of the central rules of modern narrative, what J. W. Beach called the "disappearance" of the narrator. Large portions of third-person narratives in *Nine Stories* consist of dialogue like the following:

> A woman's voice came through. "Muriel? Is that you?"
> The girl turned the receiver slightly away from her ear. "Yes, Mother. How are you?" she said.

"I've been worried to death about you. Why haven't you phoned? Are you all right?"

"I tried to get you last night and the night before. The phone here's been—"

"Are you all right, Muriel?"

Here the technique of "external focalization" severely limits the reader's access to the fictional world. He gets to know only what an impersonal medium, such as a camera or a microphone, might record. This technique stands in stark contrast to the point of view adopted in *The Catcher in the Rye*: there the use of "internal focalization" puts the reader into Holden Caulfield's mind, creating the impression of a subjective or a "figural" perspective.

The scenic presentation of Muriel Glass's phone call to her mother gives a strong sense of immediacy, especially when direct speech is not interrupted by inquits like "he said." The particles of report interspersed in the conversation are restricted to neutral descriptions of events. So the reader can be left with the illusion that he is a direct witness to the scene.

—Barbara Korte, "Narrative Perspective in the Works of J. D. Salinger," *Literatur in Wissenschaft und Unterricht* 20, no. 2 (1987): 343

ALAN NADEL ON RHETORIC, SANITY, AND THE COLD WAR IN HOLDEN CAULFIELD'S TESTIMONY

[Nadel provides historical background for certain early events of the Cold War, roughly the time Salinger was moving from writing short stories to the full-length novel *Catcher in the Rye*. Nadel discusses Salinger's opinions of Hollywood.]

Not surprisingly, Caulfield too equates Hollywood with betrayal and prostitution. The prostitute who comes to his room, furthermore, tells him she is from Hollywood, and when she sits on his lap, she tries to get him to name a Hollywood name: "You look like a guy in the movies. You know. Whosis. *You* know who I mean. What the heck's his name?" When Caulfield refuses to name the name, she tries to encourage him by associating it with that of another actor: "Sure you know. He was in that pitcher with Mel-vine Douglas. The one that was Mel-vine Douglas's kid brother. *You* know who I mean." In 1951, naming that name cannot be innocent, because of its associations. Douglas, a prominent Hollywood liberal (who in 1947 supported the Hollywood Ten and in 1951 distanced himself from them) was, more importantly, the husband of Helen Gahagan Douglas, the Democratic Congresswoman whom Richard Nixon defeated in the contest for the California Senate seat. Nixon's race, grounded in red-baiting, innuendos, and guilt by association, attracted national attention and showed, according to McCarthy biographer David Oshinsky, that "'McCarthyism' was not the exclusive property of McCarthy."

If Caulfield is guilty by virtue of his association with Melvyn Douglas, then guilty of what? Consorting with prostitutes? Naming names? Or is it of his own hypocrisy, of his recognition, also inscribed in his rhetoric, that he hasn't told the truth in that he actually loves the movies, emulates them, uses them as a constant frame of reference. The first paragraph of the book begins "if you really want to know the truth" and ends with the sentences: "If there's one thing I hate, its the movies. Don't even mention them to me." Despite this injunction, Caulfield's speech is full of them. He acts out movie roles alone and in front of others, uses them as a pool of allusion to help articulate his own behavior, and goes to see them, even when he believes they will be unsatisfactory.

—Alan Nadel, "Rhetoric, Sanity, and the Cold War: The Significance of Holden Caulfield's Testimony," *The Centennial Review* 32, no. 4 (Fall 1988): 360–61

CHARLES V. GENTHE ON SIX, SEX, SICK: SEYMOUR, SOME COMMENTS

[Genthe finds every possible reference to the number six to justify its connection to "Little Black Sambo," the story that Seymour and Sybil talk about on the beach in "A Perfect Day for Bananafish."]

In the deluge of Salinger criticism the critics have spoken learnedly of Rilke, Dostoyevsky, Twain and Buddha, they have fallen over crazy cliffs and looked intently through dark glasses hoping to see more literary allusions; but, they have neglected "Little Black Sambo." Poor "Sambo," suffering the curse of the academically forgotten, silently holds an important key to "A Perfect Day for Bananafish."

Sybil (the prophetess) Carpenter, the yellow bathing suit-clad little girl in "Bananafish," gives a veiled clue to the story's meaning. The prophetess speaks:

> "Did you read 'Little Black Sambo'?" she said. "It's very funny you asked me that," he said. "It so happens I just finished reading it last night." He reached down and took back Sybil's hand. "What did you think of it?" he asked her. "Did the tigers run all around that tree?" "I thought they'd never stop. I never saw so many tigers." "There were only six," Sybil said. "*Only* six!" said the young man. "Do you call that *only*?"

The number six is an important key to "Bananafish's" interpretation, and, indeed, to the moral and psychological problems of Seymour. As a matter of fact, there are really four tigers, not six, in the children's "Sambo." Salinger had made a change, and we can trust that it is a conscious and not inadvertent change. For Salinger, the apostle of salvation by child (NB: *The Catcher in the Rye*; "Uncle Wiggily in Connecticut," "Down by the Dingy;" "For Esmé—with Love and Squalor") would hardly inadvertent make such an error.

In "Bananafish" (1948), Seymour and Muriel Glass have been married for six years, a fact not revealed in Salinger's gradual unfolding of the Glass family's chronicle until *Raise High the Roof Beam, Carpenters* (1955). Seymour is the most admirable character in Salinger's fiction, a fact well developed in Salinger's latest efforts, for in him is combined the intellect of a genius and the moral sensitivity and compassion of a Buddhist monk; his six years with Muriel ("Miss Spiritual Tramp of 1948") have been a failure. The marriage has been six years of tigerish pride, vanity, and selfishness, in which their souls and the spiritual communion of their marriage have melted, like Sambo's tigers, into rancid nothingness.

—Charles V. Genthe, "Six, Sex, Sick: Seymour, Some Comments," *Twentieth Century Literature* 10, no. 4 (January 1965): 170–71

GARY LANE ON SEYMOUR'S SUICIDE

[Gary Lane finds elements of the German poet Rainer Maria Rilke's *Duino Elegies* in the personality of Seymour Glass. According to Lane, Seymour is an exemplar for human suffering, created by the gap between aspiration and possibility.]

Seymour Glass is the Emersonian poet, the man who "turns the world to glass" and, like Seymour in Florida, "must pass for a fool and a churl for a long season"; he is the sensitive barometer of the weather of human possibility, and the conditions he reacts against are irreversible. Perhaps he is as well Wallace Stevens' "impossible possible philosopher's man,"

> The man who has had the time to think enough,
> The central man, the human globe, responsive
> As a mirror with a voice, the man of glass,
> Who in a million diamonds sums us up.

Sybil, bright with innocence but already tarnishing, symbolizes for Seymour the human condition: like the sibyls of old, she is the unconscious oracle through whom prophecy is revealed, the instrument of truth; what she reveals to Seymour is the finality of that unbridegable gap between human aspiration and human possibility. Seymour's suicide is his summing up.

In part, he would escape the pain that his tattoo, his finite human body, invokes. For this reason Salinger emphasizes it in the final elevator vignette; the lady with the zinc salve on her nose, like Sybil's and Muriel's mothers and like the daughters themselves, is, however worldly, simple in her failure to suffer. And Seymour, who cannot resent this in a child, is understandably offended when the child-woman rudely reminds him of his pain. But the suicide is also a freeing of the self, for death has its Rilkean, life-extending properties. Seymour's final glance at Muriel—with its echo of a relationship that has failed for him because

> Eines ist, die Geliebte zu singen. Ein anderes, wehe,
> jenen verborgenen schuldigen Fluss-Gott des Bluts.
> (One thing to sing the beloved, another, alas!
> that hidden guilty river-god of the blood.)

—confirms the hopelessness of his mortal plight; for to love as a man is merely to remind oneself of the limitations of that love. Yet the glance may offer a kind of hope, for perhaps on that shadowy, darker side of life—death—human limitation will give way to infinite possibility. There is little, really, for Seymour to lose. So "he went over and sat down on the unoccupied twin bed, looked at the girl, aimed the pistol, and fired a bullet through his right temple."

—Gary Lane, "Seymour's Suicide Again: A New Reading of J. D. Salinger's 'A Perfect Day for Bananafish'" *Studies in Short Fiction* 10, no. 1 (Winter 1973): 32–33

DALLAS E. WIEBE ON SEYMOUR'S FOOT FETISH

[Wiebe contends that the bananafish are really "a foot in the sand with the toes protruding." Wiebe believes that because Seymour has abnormal feet, he commits suicide.]

Almost every commentator on the fiction of J. D. Salinger mentions "the sound of one hand clapping." Yet how few of them actually hear it! A good example of that deafness is William Wiegand's "Seventy-Eight Bananas" (in Henry A. Grunwald, ed., *Salinger: A Critical and Personal Portrait,* New York, 1962, pp. 123–36). He speaks of "banana fever" but he never defines a bananafish, a definition which is the crux of Salinger's story, "A Perfect Day for Bananafish." It is the fact that Sybil sees one with six bananas in its mouth that precipitates Seymour Glass's suicide.

When Seymour defines a bananafish for Sybil, the reader cannot know what he is talking about. It seems purely fanciful. However, what is it that Sybil actually sees when her head goes into the water? Or, what is it that Seymour thinks she sees? What she sees or what Seymour thinks she sees, is his foot in the sand. Things fall into place. The reader realizes that the description of a bananafish is actually the description of a foot in the sand with the toes protruding. That is why Seymour is touchy about his feet in the elevator. For despite the fact that he says he has two normal feet, he has, or thinks that other people think he has, six toes on one of his feet.

That deformity is as real to him as his non-existent tattoo. Suddenly Seymour realizes his abnormality and he shoots himself. Seymour has a foot fetish. He grabs and holds Sybil's ankles several times and he kisses her foot when she reports sighting a bananafish. It is, however, the number six that forms the mystical union of the story. It first appears in the story of Little Black Sambo, which may be the reason Sybil gives six as the number of bananas in the mouth of the bananafish. After that, Seymour returns to his room, number 507, and shoots himself with a 7.65 Ortgies automatic. It's as simple as hearing the one hand clapping, a left hand that of course has two thumbs.

—Dallas E. Wiebe, "Salinger's 'A Perfect Day for Bananafish,'" *The Explicator* 23, no. 1 (September 1964): item 3

WILLIAM WIEGAND ON THE CURES FOR BANANA FEVER

[Author of *The Treatment Man* and *At Last, Mr. Tolliver,* William Wiegand connects the bananafish image to images in Salinger's other short stories. Wiegand maintains that Connecticut is like the beach in "A Perfect Day for Bananafish," that is, a place away from adult realities where only memories or fantasies are at play. Eloise suffers as much as Seymour does; she agonizes because she cannot recreate her dead lover the way her daughter Ramona can invent a new imaginary friend.]

"Raise High the Roof Beam, Carpenters" affirms the bananafish in spite of the fact that the reader knows that Seymour Glass is to end as Teddy did, embracing death. Its very title, first of all, is a paean for the bridegroom, a singularly appropriate symbol for all the Salinger heroes, who are young people, people uninitiated, unconsummated, unassimilated. The story thus is a celebration of experiences, rather than a dirge for them. Moreover, it celebrates for the first time the sensitivity of the hero, marking perhaps a final surrender of the author's identification with the hero and a beginning of appreciation for him. If Seymour is a sick man, he is also a big man, and that becomes an important thing here.

While the story explains the suicide of Seymour in "Bananafish," it also makes that suicide seem a little irrelevant. It is Seymour's life, his unique way of looking at things that concerns Salinger here, and although he is obliged to mention the subsequent death of Seymour early in the story, he refers to it simply as "death," rather than a suicide. For a change, the remark seems incidental, rather than a calculated understatement, the device Salinger consistently uses when he talks about what touches him particularly.

Concerned with Seymour's life rather than with his death, Salinger is at last able to expose the bananafish here. Banana fever no longer seems the shame that it did in "Pretty Mouth," "The Laughing Man," "For Esmé" and in "A Perfect Day for Bananafish" itself, where Seymour can express himself only to a little girl, and ambiguously at that. The secretly prying eyes of others he is unable to bear. Witness the curious scene on the elevator when he accuses a woman of staring at his feet. This happens less than a minute before he puts a bullet through his head.

In "Raise High the Roof Beam, Carpenters," the frank advocacy of Seymour enables Salinger to transcend the limits of the tight pseudo-poetic structure which hamstrings so much of modern short fiction. Because the story is partisan, it must be analytic as well as metaphoric. No longer deceived into thinking his characters are prey to simple grief or to bourgeois insensitivity, rather than to beauty, he is able to expose them at last. The loosening of form, which begins with "Esmé," culminates with Seymour's throwing the stone at Charlotte, the affirmation of the effort for expression and communication even at the expense of exposure and pain.

The problem recurs in the next story, "Uncle Wiggily in Connecticut," but not without growing evidence that Salinger is ready to resist the easy answer that the bourgeoisie and/or the war is responsible for the bananafish's condition. Here, for example, it is quite clear that it is Eloise Wengler's tormenting memories of her lost lover, Walter, that make her unable to swim out of the cave into her proper place in Exurbia. Although "the war" is a factor in her despair, since her lover is killed in it, he dies not in battle but in an "absurd" camp accident; likewise, her militantly bourgeois husband may contribute to her unhappiness, but she is allowed to repay him in kind. No mere victim of society, Eloise is a bitch, not only with her husband, but with her daughter and her maid as well. She takes the revenges of an invalid.

This story contains the first clear explanation of banana fever: it is the sense of what is missing that causes suffering. Here, the lover's death brings the loss. Death, of course, is the most primitive way of making loss concrete; it is the villain of the war stories and it is still the villain here. In "Uncle Wiggily," however, we have Salinger's first sign of awareness that this sense of loss ought to be overcome; the first sign, in other words, that remembering too much is a bad thing. Eloise, for example, resents her daughter's habit of inventing invisible playmates, Mickey Mickeranno and Jimmy Jimmereeno, to take to bed with her at night. Unconsciously, Eloise knows that Walter, her lost lover, is as invisible as Ramona's boyfriends. She forces Ramona to move into the middle of the bed to prevent her daughter from lying with an invisible lover as she has had to lie with one in the years since Walter's death. She knows the consequences: her bitchiness.

These "consequences" show that Salinger was not yet willing to settle completely for a story about somebody with banana fever. In the war, he learned that actions not only had social causes but also social consequences, so he must indicate that Eloise's unhappiness affects others. In this way he absolved himself from having written an isolated, clinical report about one of the hypersensitive.

After "Uncle Wiggily," the desire to blame somebody or something generally vanishes. No longer was the evil out there somewhere; rather it was a microbe within us. We were not oppressed; we were sick.

—William Wiegand, "The Cures for Banana Fever," *Salinger: A Critical and Personal Portrait*, ed. Henry Anatole Grunwald (New York: Harper and Bros., 1962), pp. 127–28, 132–33

Critical Views on
"Uncle Wiggily in Connecticut"

BERNICE GOLDSTEIN AND SANFORD GOLDSTEIN ON ZEN
IN THE *NINE STORIES*

[In one of the many studies on Zen imagery in the work of
Salinger, the Goldsteins contrast the innocence of Ramona
to the perpetual suffering of her mother, Eloise. Eloise's
dead lover, Walt, is another character on the way to Zen
enlightenment, but Eloise is left behind in the nonaware
world of comfortable suburbia.]

In those children whose imaginative machinery has not yet been
broken by demanding parents, in those children who do not yet
rationalize every action, whose transitions jerk joyfully from one
point to another without self-consciousness or even with revenge or
demonic joy, in those children whose spontaneity comes as easily as
breath and whose minds have not yet dichotomized language, persons, places, things—to these children belong that state of enlightenment which the struggle with *koan* leads to.

The example in *Nine Stories* which readily comes to mind is
"Uncle Wiggily in Connecticut." The child Ramona with her child-
like spontaneous imaginative power is on the verge of having these
qualities eradicated by her mother, ironically referred to as "Uncle
Wiggily." It is Ramona who scratches when she feels like scratching,
who picks her nose when the nose demands picking, and who can
easily murder her latest "invisible" companion, Jimmy Jimmereeno.
Yet, it is Ramona who wears glasses, a Ramona whose vision of some
other world is so concrete that even as she sleeps, she leaves room in
bed for her "imaginary" playmate, a playmate so "real" that it walks
with her, has a sword, and is without freckles. Eloise's symbolic gesture at the end of the story, a gesture that finds her replacing her
daughter's glasses lens down—the child herself had set them down
carefully, "folded neatly and laid stems down"—reveals the lack of
vision of the adult whose perpetual conflict is her marriage to her
husband and the death of the spontaneous Walt. Eloise vividly
recalls an occasion when, on the train from Trenton to New York,
Walt had placed his hand on her stomach. This Zenlike irrational

gesture after a moment of insight is indicated when Eloise says: "All of a sudden he said my stomach was so beautiful he wished some officer would come up and order him to stick his other hand through the window. He said he wanted to do what was fair. Then he took his hand away and told the conductor to throw his shoulders back. He told him if there was one thing he couldn't stand it was a man who didn't look proud of his uniform."

The puzzle to western readers may arise when Eloise says Walt "wanted to do what was fair." Being fair from a Zen point of view is not to separate joy from pain; it means that "beauty" or "pain" or "death" or "sorrow" is not a separate category in which things, moments, persons are given names, are described by adjectives. Walt is well on the road to awareness. The state of being a general in the army does not, to Walt's way of thinking, indicate five stars but nakedness with a small infantry button stuck in the navel. That is to say, to be at the "heights" from the Zen point of view is to reduce the self to its barest quality of identity with all things, all beings. The navel suggests the position in meditation where the discursive intellect can no longer intrude.

—Bernice Goldstein and Sanford Goldstein, *"Zen and Nine Stories,"*
Renascence 22, no. 4 (Summer 1970): 172–73

RUTH PRIGOZY ON SALINGER'S LINKED MYSTERIES

[Prigozy compares the narrative points of view in "Uncle Wiggily in Connecticut" and "A Perfect Day for Bananafish," maintaining that Salinger uses visual details, such as Ramona's glasses and myopia, to lead the reader to consider other, more hidden, meanings.]

"Uncle Wiggily in Connecticut," is structured by time and place, its three sections occurring on a winter afternoon in a wealthy Connecticut suburb. That time is a major issue becomes apparent as Eloise and Mary Jane, her guest, recall their past college days, leading Eloise to recount the tragic event in her past that has corroded her present life as suburban wife and mother. As the two women drink from afternoon into evening, Eloise shows increasing nastiness, exacerbated by the tearful revelation of her lover's violent and senseless death. She expresses her unhappiness in cruel and insensitive remarks to and about her child, in a brusque drunken response to her husband's telephone call (rejecting her maid's request that her husband be allowed to spend the night because of the bad weather), and in a furious heaving of one of her daughter's galoshes over the banister. Eloise's violent and tragic story repeats itself in her daughter Ramona's imaginative life: The child kills her imaginary companion, Jimmy Jimmereeno. The emotional ending of the story—Eloise's refusal to countenance Jimmy's replacement, Mickey Mickeranno, her tears that wet the lenses of Ramona's glasses, her kiss for the sleeping child, and her final pitiful plea for reassurance that she once was a "nice girl"—fail to alleviate the pervasive bitterness of the narrative tone.

As in "A Perfect Day," the narration is informally omniscient, with an opening description that cruelly mimics the banality of Mary Jane's speech and the bitchiness of Eloise's response to Mary Jane's verbal mistake ("Merrick"): "*Merritt* Parkway, baby." Eloise is immediately identified as someone who does not allow anyone to escape her criticism. Linguistic patterns are again both subtle and obvious: Eloise never addresses Ramona by name, and she is consistently critical and irritable as when she takes the child's galoshes off: "Gimme your foot . . . Sit down, first, please. . . . Not *there—here*. God!" Eloise censures and corrects; she is unresponsive, indeed blind, to her daughter's obvious loneliness and misery. Ramona's eyes, her glasses and myopia, are linked by contrast, with Sybil's unknowingly wise misuse of Seymour's name. Salinger's language again points the reader toward meanings that lie beneath a very detailed and visually explicit surface. Here again the key moments revolve around an adult and a child and stand in sharp contrast to the affectionate exchange between Seymour and Sybil. The juxtaposition of these two stories reinforces the importance Salinger attaches to relations between adults and children.

—Ruth Prigozy, "Nine Stories: J. D. Salinger's Linked Mysteries," *Modern American Short Story Sequences: Composite Fictions and Fictive Communities,* ed. J. Gerald Kennedy (New York: Cambridge University Press, 1995), pp. 119–120

WARREN G. FRENCH ON THE PHONY WORLD AND THE NICE WORLD

[French considers the Puritanical traditions that Salinger over-comes by juxtaposing the "nice" world of Connecticut with the "phoniness" of Eloise's life in the suburbs. French believes that Salinger in "Uncle Wiggily" emphasizes the "indifference of the universe to man's ideas of good and evil."]

Why, however, is the "phony" world able to triumph over the "nice" world? "Uncle Wiggly in Connecticut" is distinctive among Salinger's work in that it is one of the few stories in which the author answers the questions about the reasons for the triumph of "phoniness" that so much distress Holden Caulfield. Salinger has not been the first to lament worldly corruption of innocence, but mourners have been divided about the reasons for the prevalence of evil. Some have placed the blame on human nature; others, on social institutions. Does Salinger embrace some kind of Puritanical notion of original sin or does he share a Rousseauistic faith in a natural goodness that social institutions have corrupted? Salinger has been cagey about showing his hand; but an answer is provided by "Uncle Wiggily in Connecticut," which pictures a person who has once been "nice" after her fall. Why couldn't Eloise remain in the "nice" world?

If she or Walt had destroyed their chances by their own misdeeds, they would indeed serve as illustrations of human depravity and Salinger would be linked to the Puritanical tradition. If, on the other hand, Walt had been killed by enemy action—or even in line of duty during the war, a savage society (what James Joyce calls "the old sow that devours its farrow") would be the culprit and Salinger might be ranked among Angry Young Rousseauists.

Walt, however, is killed neither by his own misdeeds nor the delib-erate malice of society. Eloise thus hysterically describes what did happen:

> . . . 'his regiment was resting someplace. It was between battles or something, this friend of his said that wrote me. Walt and some other boy were putting this little Japanese stove in a package. Some colonel wanted to send it home. Or they were taking it *out* of the package to rewrap it—I don't know exactly. Anyway, it was full of gasoline and junk and it exploded in their faces. The other boy just lost an eye'.

On the surface, the incident seems simply to have been a freak accident—an irrational or what the existentialists might call an "absurd" occurrence. Walt seems the victim neither of divine wrath nor of social injustice. Salinger's having him killed by a freak accident in a rest camp rather than in action deliberately emphasizes the indifference of the universe to man's ideas of good and evil. The author seems here to embrace a notion much like that expressed in Stephen Crane's ironic little poem from the "War Is Kind" group:

> A man said to the universe:
> "Sir, I exist!"
> "However," replied the universe,
> "The Fact has not created in me
> A sense of obligation."

Man, according to this theory, is simply at the mercy of the chaotic forces of blind chance. Another indication that Salinger accepts the idea of an "absurd" universe is the "senseless" death of Holden Caulfield's talented and likeable brother Allie.

—Warren G. French, "The Phony World and the Nice World," *Wisconsin Studies in Contemporary Literature* 4, no. 1 (Winter 1963): 26–27

Critical Views on
"The Laughing Man"

Richard Allen Davison on a Case of Arrested Development

[In one of the few critical analyses of "The Laughing Man," Davison reviews the "rather sparse commentary" and then offers a closer scrutiny of the story, touching on, among other issues, the ambivalent nature of Mary Hudson, the relationship between John Gedsudski and the boys in the Comanche Club, and the parallels between John and the Laughing Man.]

At the risk of running counter to this gathering trend in Salinger scholarship and criticism, I will focus my own remarks on an earlier story that seems to predate Salinger's obsession with Eastern thought, a story that has been pretty much neglected. For even during the bullish days of the Salinger Industry "The Laughing Man" never received the attention it deserves. Unlike the vastly more popular "A Perfect Day for Bananafish" (January 31, 1948), "For Esmé—with Love and Squalor" (April 8, 1950), and "Teddy" (not to mention "Uncle Wiggily in Connecticut," "Just Before the War with the Eskimos," "Pretty Mouth and Green My Eyes," "Down at the Dinghy," and "De Daumier Smith's Blue Period"), "The Laughing Man" does not have a single article devoted exclusively to it. I hope in this essay to fill some of that relative void and perhaps open a fresh discussion of Salinger's "realistic" short stories before they are buried in an avalanche of criticism on the so-called "neo-romantic" works.

To provide a clearer context for my discussion, a brief review of the rather sparse commentary on "The Laughing Man" is in order. One discovers that even the book-length studies of Salinger do not feature "The Laughing Man," although it is in Gwynn and Blotner and French that we find some of the most helpful (albeit brief) discussions of this story, which was first published in *The New Yorker* (March 19, 1949) and later became the fourth collected in *Nine Stories* (1952). Gwynn and Blotner open their two and a half page discussion with high praise: "Apparently simple, it turns out to be one of the most sophisticated and intricate of all Salinger's tales." It is judged "a great improvement over its ridiculous and distant source, Victor Hugo's *L'Homme Qui Rit* (1869)." They correctly see Salinger's story as "the recollection by a mature man of a crucial experience at the age of nine: the end of a hero-worship-laden relationship with an idealized older man"; but they wholly ignore the agonizing problems of "that older man," the twenty-two or twenty-three-year-old law student and coach to twenty-five adolescent members of the Comanche Club. George Steiner in "The Salinger Industry" first calls "The Laughing Man," along with "Down at the Dinghy," ". . . fine sketches of the bruised, complicated world of children," but then adds that "neither holds a candle to Joyce's 'Araby' or to the studies of childhood in Dostoyevsky." Adult implications are again all but ignored. William Wiegand claims that Salinger is seeking the remedy from banana fever (a central consideration of the adult-centered "A Perfect Day for Bananafish") in "The Laughing Man" through "sublimation in art." Only in "Raise High the Roof Beam" is Salinger ". . . at last able to expose the bananafish. . . . Banana fever no longer seems the shame it did in 'Pretty Mouth,' 'The Laughing Man,' 'For Esmé,'" and in 'Perfect Day' . . . itself . . . " In "The Rare Quixotic Gesture" Ihab Hassan treats Gedsudski's story of the Laughing Man (a story within a story) astutely but summarily: "Here the story of the fabulous Laughing Man is itself a quixotic gesture which has the power to influence the youthful audience of the boys, including the narrator of Salinger's story, but is powerless to save Gedsudski." Hassan doesn't explore why Gedsudski is not saved. Most of the remaining critics evidence either diminished concern with the story or a lessened ability to deal with it. This is certainly true of the essays gathered in the seven collections of Salinger criticism.

—Richard Allan Davison, "Salinger Criticism and 'The Laughing Man': A Case of Arrested Development," *Studies in Short Fiction* 18, no. 1 (Winter 1981): 3–5.

WARREN FRENCH ON "THE LAUGHING MAN"

[French discusses the effect of the break-up between Mary and John on the young narrator, and relates the symbolic mask that John wears to the "epiphany" the narrator experiences at the end of the story.]

The story at first seems unsatisfactory because the young narrator cannot tell what has happened between Gedsudski and Mary and the reader can think of not too few but of too many possible explanations. Knowing the cause of the lover's quarrel is, however, irrelevant to understanding the story; for it does not concern the romantic break-up, but the effects of this break-up on the impressionable young narrator: he suffers the double disillusionment of seeing the man he idolizes frustrated and of losing a source of innocent pleasure with the abrupt ending of the story about the laughing man. Gwynn and Blotner are mistaken when they assert that this story marks "a complete change in theme and technique" from previous *New Yorker* contributions. Like both "Uncle Wiggily in Connecticut" and "Just Before the War with the Eskimos" (and also "Blue

Melody"), "The Laughing Man" concerns the disillusioning effect upon a child of adult pettiness that the child cannot comprehend.

The precise motive for dramatizing these particular recollections, however, is obscure because Salinger does not make clear whether Gedsudski is aware of the effect that his abrupt ending of the fantastic tale has upon his young charges. If he is deliberately relieving his own frustrations through the process of displacement (by taking out upon the "Comanches" feelings that he cannot vent upon the girl who has caused them), Wiegand is correct in asserting that the tale-teller achieves a "sublimation in art." On the other hand, Hassan's explanation that art is powerless to heal is correct if Gedsudski's romantic frustration has caused him to eschew both romance and storytelling in the future. In either case, however, he is a man who will sacrifice children's feelings in order to salve his own wounds. We even wonder if Mary Hudson may not have broken with Gedsudski because she has detected beneath the mask of his superficial good fellowship the inner ruthlessness that motivates the self-made man. If so, the story is actually a bitter fable of the disillusionment of misplaced hero worship; and it is this interpretation that would make the story into the most effective account of youth's initiation into the disillusioning realities of life.

This interpretation is supported by an examination of the "epiphany" that occurs after the narrator leaves the bus and sees the piece of red tissue paper flapping against the lamppost. Since it is the sight of this discarded paper that recalls the laughing man's mask and not the abrupt ending of the story in the bus that sets the young man's teeth chattering, events in both Gedsudski's story and real life have combined to rip away a child's illusions about the real world. The tone of the narration, however, contradicts the idea that the narrator has become disillusioned about Gedsudski, because even as a grown-up the narrator speaks so enthusiastically about Gedsudski that he seems as much a hero-worshiper when he tells the story as he was when he was nine. If the boy had been really disillusioned with Gedsudski, a more ironic tone should pervade his narration of the story. It is finally impossible to tell whether the intention is to exalt or expose Gedsudski. Possibly Salinger's feelings about his character are as ambivalent as Holden's about the movies; he may be fascinated by the very "phoniness" he wishes to detect.

—Warren French, *J. D. Salinger* (New York: Twayne, 1963), pp. 92–94

☙

Critical Views on
"For Esmé—with Love and Squalor"

WILLIAM F. PURCELL ON THE SECOND WORLD WAR AND
SALINGER'S EARLY FICTION

[Purcell contends that Salinger's early fiction offers insight
into the development of his thematic interests, including his
mastery of the teenage idiom, the contrasts he draws
between youthful innocence and phony adults, and the
effects of the Second World War.]

The twenty published but uncollected early short stories of J. D.
Salinger have remained largely ignored by critical readers. Although
these early stories may be inferior to his later works, they are nevertheless significant for the insights they offer into the development of
Salinger's literary and thematic concerns. That famous Salinger ear
for teenage idiom, the close attention to detail, the "preoccupation
with close personal relations," the dichotomy of the "nice" world of
youthful innocence versus the "phony" world of adult responsi-
bility—everything that are the marks of Salinger's achievement in
his later works—are already present and developing in the early stories. In turn, the eight stories which center around the experience of
World War II are of special significance for the insights they offer
into the impact of that experience on Salinger's developing moral
vision. In these stories we can see most clearly the crucial role that
the war played in defining the spiritual and moral crises of the early
heroes, and the implications that it has for the later ones.

In reviewing the stories that were eventually preserved in
Salinger's four books, it becomes quickly apparent that none, with
the notable exception of "For Esmé—With Love and Squalor,"
openly draws upon the war for its primary themes. Of those
remaining few in which the war does appear at all, it is mostly as a
dark event lurking somewhere in the backgrounds of the main characters. Although the war does not directly enter into most of these
later stories, its impact is still evident. It is there, as James Lundquist
has said, in the form of "a mood that seemed to have affected"
Salinger, "a mood of loneliness, isolation, ineffectuality, and a sense
of being a misfit in an unfit society". His stories deal with the col-

lapse of idealism and the seemingly futile struggle to preserve youthful innocence in the face of dire adversity. Relationships, especially male-female relationships, are stunted. Communication breaks down. The characters are often confused to the point of desperation. These are the traits that mark the crises of Holden Caulfield (*The Catcher in the Rye*), of Seymour ("A Perfect Day for Bananafish," etc.) and Franny Glass ("Franny" and "Zooey"), and of all of Salinger's characters as each confronts the disenchantment of a less-than-ideal world in which circumstances lay beyond their control and deny their idealistic expectations. These are also the same problems which began emerging in those early stories that he wrote as a young soldier confronting World War II.

—William F. Purcell, "World War II and the Early Fiction of J. D. Salinger," *Studies in American Literature* 28 (February 1992): 77–78

JOHN ANTICO ON PARODY IN J. D. SALINGER

[John Antico briefly reviews commonly held interpretations of "For Esmé—with Love and Squalor" to set the stage for his counterargument. He explains why he believes that the story is really a parody of salvation at the hands of "the Girl Back Home."]

The usual interpretation of "For Esmé" has it that the love of a thirteen-year-old English girl reaches through the squalor of war to cure the war-weary Sergeant who is on the point of a nervous breakdown. Critics are often quite effusive over the power of love in the story. Although George Steiner has some reservations about Salinger's talent, he calls "For Esmé" "a wonderfully moving story" and emphasizes "the mending power of a general, nonsexual love." Ihab Hassan goes even further and calls it "a modern epithalamium," referring to its "unabashed lyricism" to which "one can only respond joyously." Although other critics may not sing the praises of the power of love as lyrically as Steiner and Hassan, with a few exceptions most critics regard "For Esmé" as one of Salinger's better stories and accept the interpretation stated above. Such an interpretation, however, makes of the story the "popular little tearjerker" that Leslie Fielder calls it, but my contention is that this is not what Salinger intended. A careful examination of the story will demonstrate that "For Esmé" is a parody of the typical sentimental war story in which the Love of The Girl Back Home boosts the Morale of the Intrepid War Hero and Saves him from Battle Fatigue. Instead of Esmé's love, it is Sergeant X's sense of humor that "saves" him; instead of an innocent, graceful, and magnanimous Esmé, we actually have a precocious snob and a cold, affected and aristocratic brat—in a word, a phony. Instead of celebrating the power of love, Salinger is satirizing what so often passes as love in bad fiction.

The story is divided into three main parts: the first is an introduction in which the narrator gives his reason for writing the story; the second is primarily about the narrator's meeting with Esmé (presumably the love part); and the third is about Sergeant X's nervous breakdown after the war and his last-minute cure (presumably the squalid part). But the story is conspicuously lacking in both love and squalor. Whatever evidence is usually cited for the "love-over-squalor" interpretation is actually irony, an irony that pervades the story from the very first sentence to the last. The reason the narrator gives for writing the story is certainly ironic. The wedding invitation from a girl the narrator met six years ago and talked to for exactly thirty minutes is a palpable absurdity. Esmé is still the pretentious, self-centered snob she was six years ago if she expects a soldier she talked to for thirty minutes during the war to travel from America to England for her wedding. After discussing the matter extensively with his wife, "a breathtakingly levelheaded girl," the narrator decides against the trip, but he is not "the type that doesn't even lift a finger to prevent a wedding from flatting," so he writes this story for Esmé. He then ends the introduction with these lines: "If my notes should cause the groom, whom I haven't met, an uneasy moment or two, so much the better. Nobody's aiming to please, here. More, really, to edify, to instruct." This is a burlesque of the inept, sentimental war story which invariably insisted on making its moralistic and pedagogical theme quite explicit as early as possible, and to take this introduction as anything but a parody is to attribute to Salinger all the marks of a tenth-rate writer of poor fiction.

—John Antico, "The Parody of J. D. Salinger: Esmé and the Fat Lady Exposed," *Modern Fiction Studies* 12, no. 3 (Autumn 1966): 326–27

[Burke suggests that "For Esmé" is really about the character of Sergeant X and not the young girl, as the title suggests. He offers, among other arguments, the contrast between Esmé and X, which is balanced by that between X and his wife and mother-in-law. In the separation from home that war creates, home can reinvent itself in other forms.]

What the title may somewhat distract from is the fact that the story has its basic unity in X. It is his story rather that Esmé's. And it is, of course, a story of character rather that incident (most of the action consists in sitting at a table and talking) and of illumination rather than of action or even of suffering. The introduction serves to characterize X in important ways for the whole story. First and most crucially, it suggests a relationship with Esmé in his response to the invitation and then contrasts this relationship with those X has with members of his own family. Secondly, it presents X as a writer. Here he has "gone ahead and jotted down a few notes" which he presents with a twist on the traditional Horatian formula: not to please but to instruct. The fact that he is a writer (with little success) will be one of the more important bits of information elicited by Esmé—and his writing of the story itself will provide the last climax in his own development. There is, thirdly, a note of self-consciousness struck in these few remarks as also in his observation that "I don't think I'm the type" and again in the intelligence hocus-pocus as he introduces the second part. As the narrative itself develops, it soon becomes evident that the main characters are extremely self-conscious, that they are, moreover, preoccupied with self-analysis and the analysis of each other, and that others are prone to analyze them, too—much of this in explicitly psychological fashion. Finally, the introduction establishes in the narrator's voice the note of an ironic, detached, but not intolerant humor—perhaps most brilliantly in his description of his wife as a "breathtakingly levelheaded girl."

It is the first element of these meanings, the relationship of characters, which provides the basic dialectic in the general structure of the story. We have seen that the introduction first suggests the relationship between X and Esmé and then contrasts this with X's relationship to his wife and mother-in-law. In the first block of the inner narrative, the dominant movement will repeat this latter relationship; it will be a movement, that is, of isolating X from those around him. The story is set in war time with D-day imminent. In this ambience the narrator presents himself as a lonely American soldier, a rather sensitive introvert who cannot find companionship among a group of other introverts who are in training with him; they are all letter-writing types who speak only "to ask somebody if he had any ink he wasn't using." His usual recreation leads him away from the group, as does his walk on the rainy Saturday on which the first part of the story takes place. After visiting the church, the soldier rejects the crowded Red Cross recreation center, enters an empty tearoom, feels snubbed by the waitress, and reads some stale letters which suggest again a lack of rapport with his relatives. Thus the basic pattern has been to isolate the hero from the country, relatives, soldier companions, the war effort itself—and, typically, to use letters and letter writing to effect that isolation.

—Brother Fidelian Burke, F.S.C., "Salinger's 'Esmé': Some Matters of Balance," *Modern Fiction Studies* 12, no. 3 (Autumn 1966): 342–43

TOM DAVIS ON THE IDENTITY OF SERGEANT X

[Davis explores the critical tendency to identify characters, to study their genealogies, and to attach autobiographical coincidences, and looks at certain parallels between Sergeant X and Seymour Glass.]

Salinger's characterization of Sergeant X and Seymour Glass reveals too many parallels to be accidental. Both have been in the army in Germany, both have been treated for mental disorders in army hospitals, both treat children as equals, and, significantly, both are married—a fact which several critics have ignored. In his essay in *Harper's*, "The Love Song of J. D. Salinger" (February 1959), Arthur Mizener suggests that Salinger "has known all about the Glasses from the beginning." And further, that "what we are told about Seymour Glass in 1948 in the first story fits precisely, both in fact and in implication with what we have learned about . . . him since." Mizener feels that most of the stories since "A Perfect Day" are related to the Glass family chronicle, and though he does not explicitly identify the "writer" in "For Esmé" with Buddy Glass, the identification is implied. Another critic, Dan Wakefield, in a *New World Writing* essay called "Salinger and the Search for Love" (December 1958), states that Buddy Glass is "the writer who appeared as 'Sergeant X.'" But if Sergeant X is a member of the Glass family, as there are many reasons for believing, then he could not be Buddy Glass. For there is an obvious fact which does not jibe with such an identification—Buddy is single. The only member of the Glass family who is married (except for Boo Boo) is Seymour. Sergeant X is Seymour Glass, and the "breathtakingly level-headed" wife and self-centered mother-in-law in "For Esmé" are Muriel Fedder Glass and her mother. Before D-Day in Normandy, for example, the mother-in-law writes to ask for some cashmere yarn; when Esmé asks Sergeant X if he loves his wife and then wonders if she is being too personal, he says he'll tell her when she becomes too personal—but he does not answer her first question. And his reply, in indirect discourse, ironically underlines the lack of love in Sergeant X's—and Seymour's—life.

If the identification of Sergeant X as Seymour Glass is correct, then one may note several things. Seymour's suicide, as seen in the light of Sergeant X's experience, is an exercise of will, and not an act of desperation. Zooey, for example, tells Franny that the first thing one must learn about the religious life is "detachment." But Seymour knows that detachment is simply another name for the "suffering of being unable to love," and that without involvement, the religious life is impossible. His marriage to Muriel was Seymour's attempt to escape the hell of detachment. Further, if the identification is correct, then Salinger's vision of Seymour is not based primarily on the Eastern concept of the oneness of things, but upon the basic dichotomies of Western fiction—right and wrong, good and evil, and, the conflict between "love and squalor." And without love, it is "a perfect day for bananafish."

—Tom Davis, "J. D. Salinger: The Identity of Sergeant X," *Western Humanities* Review 16, no. 2 (Spring 1962): 182–83

[Tosta offers a counterargument to Davis's identification of Sergeant X with Seymour Glass. He points up the discrepancies in the last names and ages of the mothers-in-law to refute Davis's position.]

In the Spring 1962 issue of *Western Humanities Review*, Tom Davis attempted to establish the identity of the Sergeant X in J. D. Salinger's "For Esmé—with Love and Squalor" as Seymour Glass, the oldest son of the Glass family and the suicide of "A Perfect Day for Bananafish." Mr. Davis presented a strong case for this theory but grounds exist for a rebuttal to this position. The most important evidence lies in the names of the mothers-in-law of both Sergeant X and Seymour Glass. In the first paragraph of "For Esmé—with Love and Squalor" the narrator writes:

> . . . I'd completely forgotten that my mother-in-law is looking forward to spending the last two weeks in April with us. I really don't get to see *Mother Grencher* terribly often, and she's not getting any younger. She's fifty-eight. (As she'd be the first to admit.) (italics added)

The Mother Grencher referred to is the mother-in-law of the narrator. When the narrator turns to telling the story of Sergeant X and Corporal Z, the narrator states the following:

> This is the squalid, or moving part of the story, and the scene changes. The people change, too. I'm still around, but from here on in, for reasons I'm not at liberty to disclose, I've disguised myself so cunningly that even the cleverest reader will fail to recognize me.

The narrator and Sergeant X are, therefore, one and the same person. This point has never been disputed by any critic.

As Mr. Davis himself states in his article, Seymour's wife is called Muriel Fedder Glass. This means that her mother's surname is Fedder, the same, naturally, as Muriel's maiden name: Muriel *Fedder*. If Sergeant X's mother-in-law is called Mother *Grencher*, she cannot be mother-in-law Fedder to Seymour Glass.

The second point in favor of such an interpretation lies in the dates of the stories. It has been stated by critics that the details of the Glass family members remain true for other stories in the Glass saga. Dates also remain consistent. The narrator of "For Esmé" relates events that took place "almost six years ago." If the events took place in April of 1944, the present time of the story would be around April of 1950. But as most readers know who have been following the Glass family stories, Seymour Glass committed suicide in 1948. Therefore, Seymour Glass could not be Sergeant X as he would not have been alive in 1950 to tell of his wartime experiences in April of 1944.

—Michael R. Tosta, "Will the Real Sergeant X Please Stand Up," *Western Humanities Review* 16, no. 4 (Autumn 1962): 376

ROBERT M. SLABEY ON SERGEANT X AND SEYMOUR GLASS

[Slabey offers a rebuttal to Davis's argument. Based on the character of Muriel Glass, Slabey contends that the narrator and Sergeant X can be one and the same but that X is not Seymour Glass because of differences in the last names of the respective mothers-in-law.]

"Sergeant X," the narrator of J. D. Salinger's "For Esmé—With Love and Squalor," is a somewhat mysterious personage. In the second half of this excellent story—"the squalid, or moving part"—he disguises himself, saying, "I've disguised myself so cunningly that even the cleverest reader will fail to recognize me." Recently (*Western Humanities Review* 16 [Spring 1962]: 181–83) Tom Davis, a reader familiar with Salinger's habit of linking his fiction, took up the challenge, identifying Sergeant X with Seymour Glass, who to date has appeared as a principle character in two stories ("A Perfect Day for Bananafish" [*The New Yorker*, 31 January 1948, and in *Nine Stories* (1953)], "Seymour: An Introduction" [*The New Yorker*, 6 June 1959]) and has been seen through other Glasses, more darkly, several times (most importantly in "Raise High the Roof Beam, Carpenters" [*The New Yorker*, 19 November 1955]). As evidence for his identification Mr. Davis cites the fact that both Sergeant X and Seymour served in the army in Germany and suffered nervous breakdowns; both find young girls attractive; and both have marital difficulties and egocentric mothers-in-law. Mr. Davis, quite cogently and correctly, makes considerable use of parallel "cat" episodes: X's collapse upon hearing his companion retell his killing of a cat with Seymour's enigmatic desire to be a "dead cat" (a Zen idea explained in "Raise High").

Additional parallels might have been suggested: Seymour had used a pseudonym ("Billy Black") on the quiz program "It's a Wise Child." Both X and Seymour are characterized by their intelligence, extreme sensitivity, and whimsical humor. The occasion for X's writing this story is Esmé's marriage; Seymour's quixotic wedding is recorded in "Raise High." At the end of "Esmé" X, his "faculties" restored, goes to sleep; at the end of "A Perfect Day" Seymour, his faculties evidently not intact, kills himself. But several significant and irrefutable differences make it infeasible to identify these two characters. Sergeant X is living in 1950 (the definite date of Esmé's wedding); but Seymour committed suicide in 1948 (the date is verified in several stories). X describes his wife as "levelheaded," while Seymour describes the rather flighty Muriel as "Miss Spiritual Tramp of 1948." X's mother-in-law is "Mother Grencher" who admits to being fifty-eight; Seymour's is Mrs. Fedder, who, from her description at least, seems to be somewhat younger. And X has an older brother in Albany; whereas Seymour is unmistakably the oldest of the seven Glass children. Sergeant X cannot be Seymour Glass, although both are avatars of the "hero" who reappears in Salinger's fiction. Salinger is fond of unifying his fiction through characters who reappear, sometimes surreptitiously, from one story to another; but present evidence makes it impossible to identify Sergeant X with Seymour Glass, the emergent focal character of the Salinger canon.

—Robert M. Slabey, "Sergeant X and Seymour Glass," *Western Humanities Review* 16, no. 4 (Autumn 1962): 376–77

JOHN WENKE ON SERGEANT X, ESMÉ, AND THE MEANING OF WORDS

[Wenke focuses on the balance that the narrator of "For Esmé" has achieved in his life after the misery he witnessed and experienced during the Second World War. Wenke believes that Salinger uses the emotional opposites of love and squalor to seek meaningful expression in life. Here, Wenke contends, emotions have precedence over words.]

In "For Esmé—with Love and Squalor," such characters as the narrator's wife and mother-in-law, Clay and Loretta, are impervious to the existential ravage inflicted by the war; others, like the soldiers in the camp and the narrator himself, perceive the bleakness of experience but can do little or nothing to overcome it or escape from it. By escaping into letter-writing, into books, or by adopting a cynical attitude, they repudiate the possibility of community and compound their isolation through acts of quiet desperation.

Nonetheless, the very fact that the story is even told in the first place suggests that there is a way to be immersed in squalor, recognize it as such, and eventually overcome it. "For Esmé" depicts extreme human misery, the suffering of being unable to love, at the same time that the narrator's very capacity to tell his story provides the completion of the psychological therapy which began when he read Esmé's letter and fell asleep. In telling the story, the narrator has clearly achieved a balance in his life, which, at the outset of the story, is implied by his good-natured, if ironic, tone. Unlike all other attempts to communicate, Esmé's letter and the process of telling the tale itself come directly out of the forces underlying their personal encounter in the Devon tearoom and possess a basis in love which is founded upon similar recognitions of the effect of squalor on the other. These acts of communication are not spontaneous emanations, but come out of periods of retrospection and consolidation during which each perceives the import of that "strangely emotional" time which they spent together. Esmé's decision to send X her father's watch could not have been hasty or gratuitous. A six year period of recovery precedes the composition of the narrator's "squalid and moving" story. For Salinger, it seems, meaningful human expression must be founded on authentic emotions which evolve into a sympathetic comprehension of another's individual needs. Forms of expression are, in themselves, neutral; they become meaningful or parodic to the extent that love or squalor resides at the heart of the relationship. The love that Salinger affirms in "For Esmé" does not depend on words, but on an emotional inner transformation which must be understood and assimilated before it can be expressed. Forms of expression cannot create love, as Clay and Loretta try to do through letters, but only express what has mysteriously been there from the start. In "For Esmé," we encounter a significant moment in Salinger's fiction, a moment during which ineffable emotional states find expression in literary forms."

—John Wenke, "Sergeant X, Esmé, and the Meaning of Words," *Studies in Short Fiction* 18, no. 3 (Summer 1981): 254

Critical Views on
"Franny"

TOM DAVIS ON THE SOUND OF ONE HAND CLAPPING

> Davis explains the relationships among Franny, Zooey, and their older siblings, Seymour and Buddy Glass. He correctly identifies the "Zooey" story as a continuation of the thought begun in "Franny," where the Jesus Prayer connects the two young Glass children to their eccentric older brothers.

In "Zooey," the story of Franny's spiritual crisis is resumed, apparently one week later. But it is incorrect, I think, to read "Zooey" as a companion piece to the earlier story simply because it resolves Franny's conflict. It is Zooey's story; and the spiritual crisis involved is as much his as Franny's, and perhaps more. Zooey's flights of wit are colored by his cynical tone and bitter remarks. About Seymour and Buddy he says:

> I'm so sick of their names I could cut my throat. . . . This whole goddam house stinks of ghosts. I don't mind being haunted by a dead ghost, but I resent like *hell* being haunted by a half-dead one.

The narrator comments that Zooey treats his mother with the "doting brutality of an apache dancer toward his partner." Franny says to Bessie Glass: "He's so *bitter* about everything." Buddy cautions him: "You demand something from the performing arts that just isn't residual there. For heaven's sake, be careful." And his mother adds: "You can't live in a world with such strong likes and dislikes." For all his precocious wit, Zooey is involved in a spiritual crisis as much as Franny. Franny's experiences have been his own— are still his own, for the world of television is the collegiate world under floodlights. Franny, with her "Jesus prayer," comes straight out of Zooey's past to upset his uneasy truce; he is compelled to think through the dark night of his own soul. And Zooey's offering is Seymour's "Fat Lady" who is, of course, "Christ Himself."

In terms of the story, the image of the Fat Lady is partly acceptable, for it apparently works for Zooey, at least where members of his own family are concerned. It also seems valid to Franny. The solution which Zooey proposes, however, is born of desperation and is his uneasy truce with a world of "writers and directors and producers" and "Mr. Tupper and his goddam cousins by the dozens."

—Tom Davis, "The Sound of One Hand Clapping," *Wisconsin Studies in Contemporary Literature* 4, no. 1 (Winter 1963): 45–46

THEODORE L. GROSS ON SUICIDE AND SURVIVAL IN THE MODERN WORLD

Gross finds merit in "Franny" and its companion text "Zooey" because he believes that Salinger finally and carefully provides a close examination of the characters, their lives, and their conflicts. Here, Gross contends that Franny solves her problems by blaming Seymour, her oldest brother.

But it is not really until the publication of *Franny and Zooey* that Salinger's central ideas assume a clear pattern and that Salinger begins an elaborate, painstaking examination of the conflict between art and life, between the poetic vision and the vanity of existence, a conflict which Seymour himself could not resolve but which the other creative members of the Glass family—writers, actors, entertainers—grow to understand as they explore the meaning of Seymour's ideas and, ultimately, of Seymour's suicide.

The tension in *Franny and Zooey* is between the idealism of Franny, expressed through the book of mysticism that she is reading, and the vulgarity of the outside world, represented in the first story by Lane Coutell and in *Zooey* by the Fat Lady. Franny rejects the reality of her particular world, those small-minded academicians who have forgotten that "knowledge *should* lead to *wisdom*" and who breed small-minded students in the form of Franny's lover, Lane Coutell. "You don't face any facts," Zooey criticizes her, and the degree to which she cannot accept the actual world, filled with people who want "to *get* somewhere, do something distinguished and all, be somebody interesting" is the degree to which she is losing her mind. Like Salinger's other characters she shuns the real world for the ideal one in her mind, represented in Franny's case by the memory of her eldest brother, Seymour.

Ultimately Franny retains her balance and achieves transcendence by referring her problem to Seymour. When Zooey despairs of helping his sister, he suggests that they try to speak to Buddy, but Franny tells him that she wants "to talk to Seymour," who of course has been dead for almost a decade and who in any case was eighteen years her senior and can now be only a dim, distorted image to her. Unable to receive direct advice from the one man who has seemed wise to her, she is nevertheless saved by Seymour through Zooey's parable of the Fat Lady. Seymour's former insistence that Zooey shine his shoes and that Franny smile for the Fat Lady—Salinger's gross symbol of humanity, suffering from boredom and cancer of the flesh and spirit—is his metaphoric way of saying that Zooey and Franny must obey the ideal in their own minds; for if the Fat Lady is Christ himself, suffering in her coarse and helpless way, and if Franny and Zooey must bring her their own finest selves, bound to the concept she embodies in whatever tenuous way, they are finally obeying the ironic name of their radio program—"It's a Wise Child"—by exhibiting wisdom, by coming to understand the suffering audience that they entertain. Wisdom is what Franny wishes, not "knowledge for knowledge's sake," and wisdom she attains, even though it appears years after she has abandoned her small role as "a wise child" and after her saintly brother has died.

—Theodore L. Gross, *The Heroic Ideal in American Literature* (New York: The Free Press, 1971), pp. 265–66

[Seed compares Franny to the little book "The Way of a Pilgrim," which acts as a buffer between Franny and Lane, her date for the weekend. Seed contends that the book is portable but Franny immobile in her ambivalence and solitude.]

Psycho-analysis is a slippery and ambiguous topic in Salinger's fiction. On the one hand (and here his fiction blends entirely into *The New Yorker* ethos of the 1940s and 1950s), it is routinely the subject of ironic jokes. On the other, Salinger clearly builds psychoanalytical subtleties into his fiction, especially the longer works of the fifties. As Seitzman notes, Lane claims not to be a "Freudian man" in explicating literature, but he then proceeds to act as an amateur psychoanalyst. This activity is complicated by the fact that he is not a disinterested party so that his amateur psycho-analysis becomes part of the overt narrative content, masking his drive for sexual supremacy. After Franny faints she comes to on the couch of the manager's office, i.e. in the posture of a patient undergoing psychoanalysis. Lane then opportunistically uses her passivity to insist on his sexual rights to her, once again partly camouflaging this pressure as concern for her physical welfare. In a sense Lane has won at the end of the novella since Franny is now entirely at his disposal, passively submissive to his plans for the rest of the day.

The one buffer against collapse which Franny carries around with her is a slim volume entitled *The Way of a Pilgrim*. Seitzman's argument would assimilate this text into Salinger's psychological themes, relating it to Franny's repressions. Given the context of allusions to psychoanalysis, it is impossible not to see the book (and the Jesus prayer it contains) in therapeutic terms. However, to do so implicates the reader in the discredited tactics of Lane and goes against the perspective of the novella itself. If Franny defines the measure of importance, then we obviously need to pin down the book's significance for her flight from self-consciousness. *The Way of a Pilgrim* is an anonymous nineteenth-century narrative of spiritual searching by a Russian who travels around the country trying to attach clear meaning to the injunction in I. Thessalonians v, 17, "pray without ceasing." Formally *The Way of a Pilgrim* contrasts strikingly with *Franny* in many respects. It is a travel-narrative where Franny herself is relatively immobile; it is punctuated by moments of insight and the seeker is guided by a religious sage, whereas Franny's insights are ambivalent, incoherent and solitary; it is also a text about *using* texts since the pilgrim carries a manual of prayer with him (*The Philokalia*), and a text for use itself, although Franny retreats behind agnosticism in the face of Lane's attacks. The particular episode which Franny describes is a meal-time scene where the pilgrim is welcomed with great hospitality. There is an obvious enough contrast here between the one scene and the situation in Salinger's novella, where Lane interrupts Franny's account by commenting on the frog's legs he is eating.

These intertextual ironies underline the pathos of Franny's predicament. and the Jesus prayer surely tantalizes her by suggesting a way in which words can be once again joined to meaning. The pilgrim's guide (the *starets*) tells him:

> Carry your mind, i.e. your thoughts from your head to your heart . . . As you breathe out, say "Lord Jesus Christ, have mercy on me." Say it moving your lips gently, or simply say it in your mind.

The prayer is partly about reforming the connections (head to heart, words to truth) which have broken in Franny's case. What fascinates her is the possibility that certain words or even a name "has this peculiar, self-active power of its own." Where she is trying to resacralize words (to use them repetitively as a kind of mantra), to Lane "God" is only available as an exclamation. Salinger carefully refuses to be explicit over Franny's degree of success here. When she moves her lips at the end of the novella, there is a clear allusion to the Jesus prayer. But equally well Franny could have lapsed into silent withdrawal.

—David Seed, "Keeping it in the Family: The Novellas of J. D. Salinger," *The Modern American Novella*, ed. A. Robert Lee (London: Vision Press, 1989), pp. 146–47

ALFRED KAZIN ON EVERYBODY'S FAVORITE

[Eminent critic Alfred Kazin observes that the best-known stories are not necessarily "first-rate pieces of literature" and focuses on Salinger's tendency to fill a scene with every possible detail. This is characteristic, Kazin contends, more of the dramatist or theater director than it is of a great novelist. Still, this tendency creates a tension that can energize each scene.]

In America, at least, where, on the whole, the best stories are the most professional stories and so are published in the most famous magazines, second-rate stories belong in the same limbo with unsuccessful musical comedies; unless you hit the bull's-eye, you don't score.

This does not mean that the best-known stories are first-rate pieces of literature any more than that so many triumphant musical comedies are additions to the world's drama; it means only that a story has communicated itself with entire vividness to its editor and its audience. The profundity that may exist in a short story by Chekhov or Tolstoy also depends upon the author's immediate success in conveying his purpose. Even in the medieval tale, which Tolstoy in his greatest stories seems to recapture in tone and spirit, the final comment on human existence follows from the deliberate artlessness of tone that the author has managed to capture like a speech in a play.

What makes Salinger's stories particularly exciting is his intense, his almost compulsive need to fill in each inch of his canvas, each moment of his scene. Many great novels owe their grandeur to a leisurely sense of suggestion, to the imitation of life as a boundless road or flowing river, to the very relaxation of that intensity which Poe thought was the aesthetic perfection of a poem or a story. But whatever the professional superficiality of the short story in American hands, which have molded and polished it so as to reach, dazzle, and on occasion deceive the reader, a writer like Salinger, by working so hard to keep his tiny scene alive, keeps everything humming.

Someday there will be learned theses on *The Use of the Ashtray in J. D. Salinger's Stories*; no other writer has made so much of Americans lighting up, reaching for the ashtray, setting up the ashtray with one hand while with the other they reach for a ringing telephone. Ours is a society complicated with many appliances, and Salinger always tells you what his characters are doing with each of their hands. In one long stretch of "Zooey," he describes that young man sitting in a bathtub, reading a long letter from his brother and smoking; he manages to describe every exertion made and every sensation felt in that bathtub by the young man whose knees made "dry islands." Then the young man's mother comes into the bathroom; he draws the shower curtains around the tub, she rearranges the medicine cabinet, and while they talk (in full), everything they do is described. Everything, that is, within Salinger's purpose in getting at such detail, which is not the loose, shuffling catalogue of the old-fashioned naturalists, who had the illusion of reproducing the whole world, but the tension of a dramatist or theater director making a fuss about a character's walking just so.

—Alfred Kazin, "Everybody's Favorite," *Salinger: A Critical and Personal Portrait*, ed. Henry Anatole Grunwald (New York: Harper and Bros., 1962), pp. 44–45

JOAN DIDION: FINALLY (FASHIONABLY) SPURIOUS

[Novelist Joan Didion takes Salinger to task for appealing to the triviality in his readers and for turning the stories of "Franny" and "Zooey" into self-help books for the upper class. She concludes that even though the prose is well rendered and the dialog possesses just the right rhythm, the text and Salinger's methodology are, in the long run, deceitful.]

What actually happens in *Franny and Zooey* is really nothing much. In "Franny," Franny Glass arrives at Princeton for a football weekend and is met by her date, strictly another of those boys with a direct wire to the PMLA, baby. He has frogs' legs for lunch and talks about Flaubert, all of which gets on Franny's nerves, especially because all she wants to do at the moment is say something called the "Jesus Prayer." ("The thing is," she explains, "the marvelous thing is, when you first start doing it, you don't even have to have *faith* in what you're doing . . . Then eventually what happens, the prayer becomes self-active. Something *happens* after a while.")

When her date somehow fails to get the point about the Jesus Prayer, Franny faints. In "Zooey," which picks up the action the next morning, we find Franny laid up at home with what her brother, a television actor named Zooey, calls "a tenth-rate nervous breakdown." She is tired of everybody's ego, not excepting her own. ("Just because I'm choosy about what I want—in this case, en*light*enment, or *peace*, instead of money or pre*stige* or *fame* or any of those things—doesn't mean I'm not as egotistical and self-seeking as everybody else.") Zooey eventually effects a cure of sorts by convincing Franny that everybody out there—no matter how given to ego, to eating frogs' legs and "*name*-dropping in a terribly quiet, *casual* voice" and wanting "to *get* somewhere"—is "Christ Himself. Christ Himself, buddy." ("Don't you know that? Don't you know that goddam secret yet?")

To anyone who has ever felt overexposed to the world, to anyone who has ever harbored hatred in his or her heart toward droppers of names, writers of papers on Flaubert, toward eaters of frogs' legs, all of this has a certain seductive lure; there is a kind of lulling charm in being assured in that dazzling Salinger prose that one's raw nerves, one's urban hangover, one's very horridness, is really not horridness at all but instead a kind of dark night of the soul; there is something very attractive about being told that one finds en*light*enment or *peace* by something as eminently within the realm of the possible as tolerance toward television writers and section men, that one can find the peace which passeth understanding simply by looking for Christ in one's date for the Yale game.

However brilliantly rendered (and it is), however hauntingly right in the rhythm of its dialogue (and it is), *Franny and Zooey* is finally spurious, and what makes it spurious is Salinger's tendency to flatter the essential triviality within each of his readers, his predilection for giving instructions for living. What gives the book its extremely potent appeal is precisely that it is self-help copy: it emerges finally as *Positive Thinking* for the upper middle classes, as *Double Your Energy and Live Without Fatigue* for Sarah Lawrence girls.

—Joan Didion, "Finally (Fashionably) Spurious," *Salinger: A Critical and Personal Portrait*, ed. Henry Anatole Grunwald (New York: Harper and Bros., 1962), pp. 78–79

[Novelist and poet John Updike claims that although the stories apparently fit together, in fact they do not. Updike concludes that Salinger pays a great deal of attention to nuance and ambiguity, and that gesture and intonation define his study of human subjectivity.]

"Franny" and "Zooey" have a book to themselves. These two stories—the first medium-short, the second novella-length—are contiguous in time, and have as their common subject Franny's spiritual crisis.

In the first story, she arrives by train from a Smithlike college to spend the weekend of the Yale game at what must be Princeton. She and her date, Lane Coutell, go to a restaurant where it develops that she is not only unenthusiastic but downright ill. She attempts to explain herself while her friend brags about a superbly obnoxious term paper and eats frogs' legs. Finally, she faints, and is last seen lying in the manager's office silently praying at the ceiling.

In the second story, Franny has returned to her home, a large apartment in the East Seventies. It is the Monday following her unhappy Saturday. Only Franny's mother, Bessie, and her youngest brother, Zooey, are home. While Franny lies sleeplessly on the living-room sofa, her mother communicates, in an interminably rendered conversation, her concern and affection to Zooey, who then, after an even longer conversation with Franny, manages to gather from the haunted atmosphere of the apartment the crucial word of consolation. Franny, "as if all of what little or much wisdom there is in the world were suddenly hers," smiles at the ceiling and falls asleep.

Few writers since Joyce would risk such a wealth of words upon events that are purely internal and deeds that are purely talk. We live in a world, however, where the decisive deed may invite the holocaust, and Salinger's conviction that our inner lives greatly matter peculiarly qualifies him to sing of an America where, for most of us, there seems little to do but to feel. Introversion, perhaps, has been forced upon history; an age of nuance, of ambiguous gestures and psychological jockeying on a national and private scale, is upon us, and Salinger's intense attention to gesture and intonation help make him, among the contemporaries, a uniquely pertinent literary artist. As Hemingway sought the word for things in motion, Salinger seeks the words for things transmuted into human subjectivity. His fiction, in its rather grim bravado, its humor, its morbidity, its wry but persistent hopefulness, matches the shape and tint of present American life. It pays the price, however, of becoming dangerously convoluted and static. A sense of composition is not among Salinger's strengths, and even these two stories, so apparently complementary, distinctly jangle as components of one book.

—John Updike, "Franny and Zooey," *Salinger: A Critical and Personal Portrait,* ed. Henry Anatole Grunwald (New York: Harper and Bros., 1962), pp. 53–54

Critical Views on
"Raise High the Roof Beam, Carpenters"

JAMES FINN COTTER ON RELIGIOUS SYMBOLISM

[Of the many symbols that Cotter considers, here he looks in particular at glass, cigars, and ashes. He attributes the same importance to ashtrays as to glass: They are "reliquaries of the godhead's immanence."]

In "Carpenters," while waiting for the parade to march by, the five passengers of the taxi express their frustration at the delay. Not the tiny, elderly uncle. He sits erect, unperturbed, staring "ferociously ahead at the windshield." Buddy observes: "If Death stepped miraculously through the glass and came in after you, in all probability you just got up and went along with him, ferociously but quietly." Again, the glass symbolizes the human condition as the locale of divine life. When the deaf-mute leaves his empty glass behind him, it is all the proof we need of his eternal existence. Except, of course, for his cigar end in the pewter ashtray.

Cigarette and cigar ashes are also *vestigia* of God's neglected presence in man's midst. The old uncle's clear Havana remains unlit until the *agape* begins, "and—lo and behold—*his cigar was lighted.*" In one of his "early-blooming parentheses," Buddy reports of Seymour: "My brother, for the record, had a distracting habit, most of his adult life, of investigating loaded ashtrays with his index finger, clearing all the cigarette ends to the sides—smiling from ear to ear as he did it—as if he expected to see Christ himself curled up cherubically in the middle, and he never looked disappointed." Seymour is searching for the *sarira* which, for Zen Buddhists, is the indestructible substance found only in the remains of cremated saints. Since God is essential reality, Seymour finds in the ashes the Christ he seeks. Zooey answers Franny's question about Boo Boo's religious philosophy with a very revealing pun: "Boo Boo's convinced Mr. Ashe made the world. She got it from Kilvert's 'Diary.'" The schoolchildren in Kilvert's parish were asked who made the world, and one of the kids answered "Mr. Ashe." The secret lay hidden in the diary of an obscure nineteenth-century pastor: God is Mr. Ashe. As Jesus promised, he abides until the end of time, but not where most people think to look. In Salinger's anti-puritanical view, Mr. Ashe lives on in the interstices and residue of man's actions, in his smoking, drinking, and swearing. *Tat tvam asi:* "That art Thou." Incarnation destroys life's seeming insignificance and leaves signs and symbols rampant in each day's incidents and details.

The many references to ashtrays in Salinger's stories support the religious significance he imparts to certain objects. Like glasses, they are reliquaries of the godhead's immanence. The *sadhu* Teddy, once again, provides the arcanum by combining both symbols when he picks up "the glass ashtray that belonged on the night table" and "swept his father's cigarette stubs and ashes" into it; then "he placed the ashtray on the glass top, with a world of care, as if he believed an ashtray should be dead-center on the surface of a night table or not placed there at all." For modern man, the divine omphalos no longer survives in one sacred spot. The artist, too, must explore new terrains for his mythmaking. Buddy recalls: "Seymour once said that all we do our whole lives is go from one little piece of Holy Ground to the next." More than ever, the ancient definition proves true: "God is a circle whose center is everywhere and whose circumference is nowhere."

—James Finn Cotter, "Religious Symbols in Salinger's Shorter Fiction," *Studies in Short Fiction* 15, no. 2 (Spring 1978): 128–29

FRANK METCALF ON THE SUICIDE OF SEYMOUR GLASS

[Metcalf discusses "Raise High the Roof Beam, Carpenters,"
"Hapworth 16, 1924," and "A Perfect Day for Bananafish" to
reveal further sexual connotations in Seymour's behavior.]
In "Raise High the Roof Beam," Buddy relates two events that
occurred when Seymour was about twelve years old, both incidents
involving a girl named Charlotte Mayhew. The first was a recurring
incident on the "It's a Wise Child" program: Charlotte tramped on
Seymour's foot when he said something she liked, and Seymour
apparently enjoyed her expressions of approval, even though they
were frequently painful. The second event is Seymour's hitting Charlotte with a rock and scarring her face, an act motivated, according
to Buddy, by Charlotte's looking beautiful while petting a cat. In
view of Seymour's sensual nature revealed in "Hapworth," it seems
to me not implausible to suggest that Seymour's enjoyment of foot-
trampling is sexual and that his attack on Charlotte is motivated by
sexual aggression. Admittedly, this is a suggestion that few Seymour
fans, Buddy among them, would care to make; but it is one that
acquires support and significance when it is considered in connection with Seymour's marriage.

The relationship between Charlotte Mayhew and Muriel Fedder is
innocently established by Mrs. Silsburn and Lieutenant Burwick.
Observing a photograph of Charlotte taken while she was on the radio
program, both notice a strong resemblance between her and Muriel.
Mrs. Silsburn, in fact, states that Charlotte is a double for Muriel at
that age. According to Buddy, her statement has "many possible rami-
fications," although he does not suggest any. The reader, however, is
free to speculate; and since I am concerned here with Seymour's
sexual adjustment, I would suggest that one ramification is that Seymour's attraction to Muriel is occasioned by sublimated pedophilic
desires. In other words, in possessing Muriel, Seymour unconsciously
is fulfilling a sexual desire for the child Charlotte Mayhew. (In making
this suggestion, I might add that I am not unaware that both Buddy
and Seymour give a reason for Seymour's attraction to "noisy girls": the
girls' love and desire for physical existence provide a necessary balance
to Seymour's love and desire for the infinite. I hope, however, that it has
not yet become an axiom of Salinger criticism that the author's inten-
tions may not be separated from the beliefs of his characters.)

By taking into account Charlotte Mayhew and the possibility of Seymour's pedophilic tendencies, one may explain the incidents of "A Perfect Day for Bananafish." The erotic trifling with Sybil which Fielder notices is not, I think, as innocently intended as he assumes, and the bananafish tale, which Irving Malin parenthetically suggests is "an anxiety-dream of a mature relationship with a woman" may rather be the statement of a repressed desire for a sexual relationship with Sybil. A number of critics have suggested that Seymour is the bananafish, but none, I think, have identified Sybil with the banana, an identification I am not in the least facetious in making: she wears a yellow bathing suit, and she has blond hair. If Sybil is identified with the banana, the sexual implications of the bananafish tale become clear. The connection between Charlotte and Sybil provides the reason for Seymour's kissing Sybil's foot: the kiss is an expression of the sexual desire aroused in Seymour by Charlotte's trampling his foot on the radio program.

— Frank Metcalf, "The Suicide of Salinger's Seymour Glass," *Studies in Short Fiction* 9, no. 3 (Summer 1972): 245–46

IHAB HASSAN ON THE VOICE OF SILENCE

[The author of *The Literature of Silence,* Ihab Hassan provides an overview of the opening narrative in "Raise High the Roof Beam, Carpenters," focusing on the confusion in the scene where Buddy is surrounded by an unfriendly group of wedding guests.]

Seymour Glass haunts all the Glass children in the later stories of Salinger. This is their central theme. Despite its hieratic connotations, the theme embodies Salinger's wider concern with the uses and communicability of love or holiness in this world. It is in his efforts to dramatize this concern that Salinger has felt the need to make the stories seem almost capricious.

"Raise High the Roof Beam, Carpenters," which first appeared in *The New Yorker,* 19 November 1955, is perhaps the least capricious of the stories. It is narrated by Buddy Glass, the family chronicler, who is born, as Salinger himself was, in 1919, and it purports to describe the circumstances of Seymour's marriage to Muriel Fedder in June of 1942. Actually, the story deals with Buddy even more than with Seymour. It begins with a prologue, set back twenty years when Seymour and Buddy were still in their teens. The prologue contains the Taoist parable of a fuel hawker who can distinguish the "good" from the "superlative" horse by focusing only on its "spiritual mechanism." Buddy concludes the epilogue thus: "Since the bridegroom's permanent retirement from the scene [i.e., Seymour's suicide in 1948], I haven't been able to think of anybody whom I'd care to send out to look for horses in his stead" (51). Buddy starts with veneration for his brother; his resentment, suppressed by love, appears later.

The prologue is followed by a wild introduction to the Glass family. The charmed solidarity of the Glasses is evoked wryly by references to the radio program, "It's a Wise Child," in which all the children participated over a span of eighteen years. When the action finally begins, it begins with a letter from Boo Boo Glass to Buddy, charging him to attend their brother's wedding. The concern for Seymour is universal in the family. Convalescing still from an attack of pleurisy, Buddy makes his way from Georgia to New York in the custody of three yards of adhesive tape around his ribs. Seymour, however, is "too happy" to attend his own wedding. The gathering breaks up. On the way out, Buddy finds himself in a limousine with four people, friends and relations of the abandoned bride. The day is blazingly hot, and the indignation of all against Seymour is explosive. This is particularly true of the Matron of Honor, a formidable, athletic, "one-woman mob." The other three are her cowed husband, a genteel aunt, and a tiny elderly man with a glossy top hat and an unlit cigar, who turns out to be a deaf-mute relative of the bride. The last is the only one to earn the boundless affection of Buddy who has not dared yet to identify himself as Seymour's brother.

Salinger, we see, has slyly created a situation rich with confusion and misunderstanding. The characters are strangers to one another. The meaning of the event they are seeking to interpret is as unknown to them as is its outcome. And the subject of calumny, Seymour, eludes them entirely. The Matron of Honor begins by accusing Seymour, on the authority of Mrs. Fedder, of being a schizoid, a latent homosexual, and a sadist, the latter being a misinterpretation of the cause of nine stitches on Charlotte Mayhew's cheek. Buddy, still anonymous, is made to experience a wave of prejudice and resentment against his brother. This leads him, in one of the numerous, formal digressions of the piece, to examine his cowardly motives for remaining in the car. His answer is this: "the year was 1942 . . . I was twenty-three, newly drafted, newly advised in the efficacy of keeping close to the herd—and, above all, I felt lonely." But the confusion of human motives is further abetted by the confusion in language. Clichés, slogans, ejaculations, second and third hand gossip, patriotic parades, bands playing raucous music, Sea Scouts singing off-key, written notes passed back and forth in the car, messages scrawled with soap on bathroom mirrors, rhapsodic entries in a private diary, and phone calls with inaudible connections, envelop reality in a sur-real haze. It is no wonder that Buddy, referring to the year 1942 for the fifth time, says, "It was a day, God knows, not only of rampant signs and symbols but of wildly extensive communication via the written word." Only the sublime silence of the little man with an unlit cigar can Buddy apprehend as communication, a voice of solace reaching into his solitude.

—Ihab Hassan, "Almost the Voice of Silence: The Later Novelettes of J. D. Salinger," *Wisconsin Studies in Contemporary Literature* 4, no. 1 (Winter 1963): 7–8

SAM S. BASKETT ON THE SPLENDID/SQUALID WORLD OF J. D. SALINGER

[Baskett examines the character of Buddy Glass in "Raise High the Roof Beam, Carpenters." He relates Buddy with Salinger and maintains that Salinger deliberately blurs the difference between character and author. Though Buddy's manner of expression is decidedly flippant, Baskett believes this is Salinger's way of emphasizing the importance of the writer's portrayal of life.]

Buddy's characterization is not always sharply defined, both because he is a partially achieved Seymour and because, as Salinger has pointedly remarked, he is really indistinguishable from the author, in essential attributes at least. Buddy-Salinger presents himself principally in three stories, "Raise High the Roof Beam, Carpenters," "Zooey," and "Seymour." In these stories Salinger seems deliberately to be blurring, in the manner of Gide, the distinction between character and author, between life and fiction, until the intrusive remarks become at least as germane and significant as the plot line. "Seymour," for example, opens with quotations from Kafka and Kierkegaard concerning the relation between an author and his characters; in fact, in this story the effort of the author to render experience into pattern actually *becomes* the plot line. Buddy writes almost flippantly of his effort to capture the word, to give the experience form, to unfold the meaning. But this flippancy does not obscure the fact that Salinger is completely serious and that he is representing Buddy as totally committed to the superlative importance and transcending difficulty of the tasks of the writer in seeing and portraying life.

Buddy is not an artist comparable to the other Sick Men (Kafka, Kierkegaard, Van Gogh, Seymour) "whom I most often run to— occasionally in real distress—when I want any perfectly credible information about modern artistic processes." Buddy's insight, his capacity, is distinctly less rarefied. Recognizing his imperfect capacities, Buddy is nonetheless dedicated to the pursuer if the understanding which the "true artist-seer" is blessed and cursed with; as Seymour writes him, "When was writing ever your profession? It's never been anything but your religion." For Buddy, and of course, for Salinger, as a writer, this pursuit means a different kind of "story" than he had written earlier: "Speed, here, God save my American hide, means nothing whatever to me." Being "no longer in a position to . . . get the hell on with his story," Buddy invites the reader primarily interested in what happens to "leave now, while, I can imagine, the leaving's good and easy."

—Sam S. Baskett, "The Splendid/Squalid World of J. D. Salinger," *Wisconsin Studies in Contemporary Literature* 4, no. 1 (Winter 1963): 58–59

Works by
J. D. Salinger

Uncollected Stories

"Go See Eddie." *University of Kansas City Review* 7 (December 1940): 121–24.

"The Young Folks." *Story* 16 (March–April 1940): 26–30.

"The Hang of it." *Collier's,* 12 July 1941, 22.

"The Heart of a Broken Story." *Esquire,* September 1941.

"The Long Debut of Lois Taggett." *Story* 21 (September–October 1942): 28–34.

"Personal Notes on an Infantryman." *Collier's,* 12 December 1942, 96.

"The Varioni Brothers." *Saturday Evening Post,* 17 July 1943, 12–13, 76–77.

"Both Parties Concerned." *Saturday Evening Post,* 26 February 1944, 14, 47–48.

"Soft-Boiled Sergeant." *Saturday Evening Post,* 26 February 1944, 18, 82, 84–85.

"Last Day of the Last Furlough." *Saturday Evening Post,* 15 July 1944, 26–27, 61–62, 64.

"Once a Week Won't Kill You." *Story* 25 (November–December 1944): 23–27.

"Elaine." *Story* 26 (March–April 1945): 38–47.

"A Boy in France." *Saturday Evening Post,* 31 March 1945, 21, 92.

"This Sandwich Has No Mayonnaise." *Esquire,* October 1945, 54–64, 147–49.

"The Stranger." *Collier's,* 1 December 1945, 18, 77.

"I'm Crazy." *Collier's,* 22 December 1945, 36, 48, 51.

"Slight Rebellion off Madison." *New Yorker,* 21 December 1946, 76–79.

"A Young Girl in 1941 with No Waist at All." *Mademoiselle,* May 1947, 222–23, 292–302.

"The Inverted Forest." *Cosmopolitan,* December 1947, 73–80, 85–86, 88, 90, 92, 95–96, 98, 100, 102, 107, 109.

"A Girl I Knew." *Good Housekeeping,* February 1948, 37, 186, 188, 191–96.

"Blue Melody." *Cosmopolitan,* September 1948, 51, 112–19.

"Hapworth 16, 1924." *New Yorker,* 19 June 1965, 32–113.

Collected Short Fiction

Franny and Zooey. Boston: Little, Brown, 1961.

Nine Stories. Boston: Little, Brown, 1953.

Raise High the Roof Beam, Carpenters and Seymour: An Introduction. Boston: Little, Brown, 1963.

Fiction

The Catcher in the Rye. Boston: Little, Brown, 1951.

Works about
J. D. Salinger

Alsen, Eberhard. "'Raise High the Roof Beam, Carpenters' and the Amateur Reader." *Studies in Short Fiction* 17 (1980): 39–47.

_____, *Salinger's Glass Stories as a Composite Novel.* Troy, NY: Whitson, 1983.

Belcher, William F., and James W. Lee, eds. *J. D. Salinger and the Critics.* Belmont, CA: Wadsworth Publishing Company, 1962.

Bloom, Harold, ed. *J. D. Salinger.* Chelsea House Books, New York, 1983.

Browne, Robert M. "In Defense of Esmé." *College English* 22 (May 1961): 584–85.

Bryan, James. "A Reading of Salinger's 'Teddy.'" *American Literature* 40 (1968): 352–69.

_____. "J. D. Salinger: The Fat Lady and the Chicken Sandwich." *College English* 23 (December 1961): 226–29.

_____. "The Admiral and Her Sailor in Salinger's 'Down at the Dinghy.'" *Studies in Short Fiction* 17 (1980): 174–78.

Dahl, James. "What about Antolini?" *Notes on Contemporary Literature* 13 (1983): 9–10.

Dodge, Stewart. "In Search of 'The Fat Lady.'" *The English Record.* 8 (Winter 1957): 10–13.

Fiene, Donald F. "J. D. Salinger: A Bibliography." *Wisconsin Studies in Contemporary Literature* 4 (Winter 1963): 109–49.

Giles, Barbara. "The Lonely War of J. D. Salinger." *Mainstream* 12 (February 1959): 2–13.

Goldstein, Bernice, and Sanford Goldstein. "Ego and 'Hapworth 16, 1924.'" *Renascence* 24 (1972): 159–67.

_____. "'Seymour: An Introduction': Writing as Discovery." *Studies in Short Fiction* 7 (1970): 248–56.

_____. "Zen and Salinger." *Modern Fiction Studies* 12 (Autumn 1996): 313-24.

Gross, T. L. "J. D. Salinger: Suicide and Survival in the Modern World." *The South Atlantic Quarterly* 68 (1969): 452–62.

Gwynne, Frederick L., and Joseph L. Blotner. *The Fiction of J. D. Salinger.* Pittsburgh: University of Pittsburgh Press, 1958.

Hagopian, J. V. "'Pretty Mouth and Green My Eyes': Salinger's Paolo and Francesca in New York." *Modern Fiction Studies* 12 (1966): 349–54.

Hamilton, Kenneth. *J. D. Salinger: A Critical Essay.* Grand Rapids: Eerdmans, 1967.

Hermann, John. "J. D. Salinger: Hello Hello Hello." *College English,* 22 (January 1961): 262–64.

Kirschner, Paul. "Salinger and His Society: The Pattern of Nine Stories." *London Review* 6 (1969): 34–54.

McIntyre, J. P. "A Preface for Franny and Zooey." *Critic* 29 (1962): 25–28.

Miller, James E. Jr. *J. D. Salinger.* Minneapolis: University of Minnesota Press, 1965.

Phillips, Paul. "Salinger's Franny and Zooey." *Mainstream* 15 (1969): 32–39.

Seitzman, Daniel. "Salinger's 'Franny': Homoerotic Imagery." *American Imago* 22 (1965): 57–76.

Sharma, Som P. Ranchan. "Echoes of the Gita in Salinger's Franny and Zooey." *The Gita in World Literature.* C. D. Verma, ed. New Delhi: Sterling, 1990.

Silverburg, Mark. "A Bouquet of Empty Brackets: Author-Function and the Search for J. D. Salinger." *Dalhousie Review* 75 (Summer–Fall 1995): 222–46.

Stein, W. B. "Salinger's 'Teddy': Tat Twam Asi or That Thou Art." *Arizona Quarterly* 29 (1974): 253–56.

Tierce, Mike. "Salinger's 'De Daumier-Smith's Blue Period.'" *The Explicator* 42, no. 1 (1983): 56–58.

Wenke, John. *J. D. Salinger: A Study of the Short Fiction.* Boston: Twayne Publishers, 1991.

Index of
Themes and Ideas

CATCHER IN THE RYE, THE, 10, 11, 42; Allie Caulfield in, 52; Holden Caulfield in, 8, 40–41, 51, 55, 57; internal focalization in, 40

"FOR ESMÉ WITH LOVE AND SQUALOR," 37, 42, 46, 54; Charles in, 19, 20, 31; Clay (Corporal Z) in, 21, 31, 62, 65; critical views on, 56–66; emotion in, 64–66; Esmé in, 18, 19–20, 21, 31, 33, 57, 58, 59, 61, 64, 65; Mother Grencher in, 18, 31, 61, 62, 64, 65; Loretta in, 21, 31, 65; Sergeant X in, 20, 21, 31, 57, 58, 59–64, 65; plot summary of, 18–21

"FRANNY": Wally Campbell in, 24; Lane Coutell in, 22–24, 32, 67, 68, 69, 72, 74; critical views on, 66–75; as deceitful, 72–73; detail in, 71–72; gesture and intonation in, 74–75; Franny Glass in, 8, 22, 23, 24, 66–68, 69–70, 72–73, 74; Jesus prayer in, 67, 70, 72; sibling relationships in, 66–67; plot summary of, 22–24; *The Way of the Pilgrim* and, 69–70

"LAUGHING MAN, THE": Black Wing in, 16, 17, 18, 30; child's disillusionment with adult pettiness in, 54–55; critical views in, 52–55; Marcel Dufarge in, 16, 17–18, 31; Mlle. Dufarge in, 16, 17–18; Eurasian girl in, 16, 30; foot imagery in, 38; John Gedsudski in, 16–17, 30, 38, 54, 55; Hong in, 16, 30; Mary Hudson in, 16–17, 30, 38, 39, 54, 55; Laughing Man in, 16, 17–18, 30, 39, 54, 55; narrator in, 15, 16–17, 18, 30, 54, 55; Omba in, 16, 18, 30; plot summary of, 15–18

"PERFECT DAY FOR BANANAFISH, A," 8, 25, 53, 54, 78; Mrs. Carpenter in, 29; Sybil Carpenter in, 13, 29, 42, 43, 44, 45, 50, 78; critical views on, 39–47; external folcalization in, 39–40; foot imagery in, 44–45, 78; Muriel Glass in, 12–13, 29, 33, 39–40, 42, 61, 62, 64; Seymour Glass in, 8, 10, 12, 13, 33, 42, 43–46, 50, 57, 78; Sharon Lipschutz in, 13; Muriel's father in, 12; Muriel's mother in, 12, 29, 33, 39–40, 43, 61, 62, 64; number six in, 41–42, 44, 45; Sivetski in, 12; plot summary of, 12–13

"RAISE HIGH THE ROOF BEAM, CARPENTERS," 8, 11, 45, 54, 63; Mr. Burwick (Lieutenant) in, 25, 26, 32, 77, 79; Mrs. Burwick (Matron of Honor) in, 25–26, 27, 32, 79; critical views on, 75–81; elderly man in, 26, 32, 79; Mrs. Fedder in, 26, 27, 32, 79; foot imagery in, 38, 77; Buddy Glass in, 25, 26, 27–28, 32, 61, 75, 76, 77, 78–79, 80–81; Muriel Fedder Glass in, 25, 26, 27, 32, 38, 39, 77, 79; Seymour Glass in, 25–26,